Praise for
An Unconventional Journey

Having been deeply touched by the "magic of Findhorn," Lisa Paulson resolved to bring it back to the American Midwest, translate it into terms that others could relate to, and work with it to create a "sustainable community" long before this became the thing to do. *An Unconventional Journey* captures the story of how High Wind pioneered the "eco-ethos" that may yet guide us toward a more sustainable world.
> — Roger Doudna, PhD, 35-year resident of the Findhorn Foundation community and coordinator of the Findhorn Foundation Fellowship

An Unconventional Journey is for dreamers or would-be dreamers. Combining her narrative with testimonies of many participants, along with lots of photos, Lisa Paulson takes you inside the High Wind community and establishes its place in those turbulent times. Her account will interest students of social history along with those who share her discontents with society. This book will be a valuable addition to your library.
> — Henry M. Halsted III, Vice President Emeritus, the Johnson Foundation, Racine, Wisconsin

Community is never easy, no matter how high the ideals. Lisa Paulson candidly describes the efforts shared with her husband in attempting to build an intentional community in Wisconsin, USA, which sought to demonstrate both eco-sustainability and spiritual growth while still attending to the very human dynamics of day to day living. Through her story, Lisa reveals the rewards as well as the deeply challenging issues which face communities in the world today. I recommend this book.
> — Dorothy Maclean, cofounder of the Findhorn Foundation community and founding member of the Lorian Association

Lisa Paulson has succeeded in conveying, in words and pictures, a good understanding of the complex phenomenon of High Wind. *An Unconventional Journey* demonstrates what can get accomplished when people join together around a shared lofty vision and purpose. It is a great inspirational and educational text for would-be community builders.
> — Harry Schwarzlander, engineer, system theorist, and futurist at Syracuse University, and founder of the New Environment Association

A true local community journalist is in a freedom business that sells credibility and uses ideas as raw material. Paulson measures up to this challenging definition in a delightfully engaging way.
> — Barry Johanson, Editor and Publisher since 1963, *The Review* (Plymouth, Wisconsin)

The Story of High Wind

From Vision to Community to Eco-Neighborhood

An Unconventional Journey

The Story of High Wind

From Vision to Community to Eco-Neighborhood

Lisa Paulson

WITH FOREWORD BY
DAVID SPANGLER

Thistlefield Books
Plymouth, Wisconsin

An Unconventional Journey, The Story of High Wind: From Vision to Community to Eco-Neighborhood
by Lisa Paulson
Copyright © 2010 by Lisa Paulson

Cover: Award-winning painting, *The Dark and the Light*, by Lisa Paulson, © 2008.
Prairie plant drawings throughout the book are by Marcia Kjos.
All photos, unless otherwise noted, are from the personal collection of the author.
The photo on page 92 of Hawthorne House interior is courtesy of Eric Oxendorf.
The photo on page 93 is by Ronald M. Overdahl and is reproduced with permission of the
     Milwaukee Journal Sentinel.
The photo of the circle dance on page 98 is by Tim Conner.
The photo on page 106 is courtesy of Dan Somsky.
The cartoon by Vaughn on page 124 was first published by *The Review* (Plymouth, Wisconsin).
The photo on page 129 is by Doug Green.
Back cover photo and photo on page 159 are with permission of Leslie Faye.

First Printing 2010
Printed in the United States of America
14 13 12 11 10   1 2 3 4 5
ISBN-13: 978-0-9816906-2-9
Library of Congress Control Number: 2010937446

Editor: Carolyn Kott Washburne
Design and Typography: Kate Hawley
Concept Development and Production Coordinator: Susan Pittelman
This book is printed on acid-free paper.

Published by Thistlefield Books
W7122 County Road U
Plymouth, Wisconsin 53073
(920) 528-8488 www.ThistlefieldBooks.com

With deep appreciation to the Findhorn community,
the New Alchemy Institute, and the Lorian Association

For Harry and Pat,
Fellow pioneers, tirelessly
spreading the values of community.
We treasure our connection!

Blessings,

Lisa

Where there is no vision, the people shall perish.

— Book of Proverbs, 29:18

An unexamined life is not worth living.

— Socrates

Without a global revolution in the sphere of human consciousness, nothing will change for the better in the sphere of our being as humans. . . . The salvation of this human world lies nowhere else than in the human heart. . . .

— Václav Havel, president of Czechoslovakia, addressing the United States Congress on February 21, 1990

Acknowledgments

Bel, always my partner, in life and in the work of creating High Wind; my perfect counterbalance, best friend, and reliable mirror as well as support;

The three hundred members of the Findhorn community in Scotland who in 1976 were living out a scenario of sustainable practices decades before most of the world caught on, and whose example—integrating spiritual, social, and ecological realms—jolted me into turning my life upside down and carrying their radical message home to America;

The New Alchemy Institute in Massachusetts, particularly its imaginative founders, John and Nancy Todd, whose vision and stunning demonstrations of groundbreaking alternative technologies inspired us to build our own experimental bioshelter at High Wind;

All the Lorian group, especially Milenko Matanovic, David Spangler, and Dorothy Maclean, mentors extraordinaires, who held our hands and guided us in the creation of High Wind, helping us over the first bumps and pitfalls with their wisdom and experience;

Angelynn Brown, my "bridge" from Findhorn, who, in our early partnership, brought depth and focus and heart to galvanize the first Wisconsin enthusiasts for our work—and who continues to be a visionary friend—as well as (now) my daughter-in-law;

Our son Eric, who, in very hands-on ways and in his unique, sensitive being, has consistently inspired and lifted whatever situation he finds himself in to another level of serenity, beauty, and harmony;

Our son Steve, my first editor, who read, wisely critiqued, and encouraged my various writing efforts from early on (while also cocking an occasional skeptical eye and asking the important tough questions);

The High Wind residents, whose spirit, wisdom, wit, vision, resilience, and tenacity carried our community through both harrowing shoals and magnificent heights—and pushed me to learn a great many lessons about myself. Particularly David Lagerman, whose fervor about living sustainably has carried High Wind from the beginning and whose renaissance qualities and personal example continue to fuel our resolve; Patti Neilon, an early cheerleader for High Wind who volunteered her skills as an artist and calligrapher in the first years to help put together our community newsletter *Windwatch,* which I edited; David Neilon, Patti's husband, who brought his entire construction crew to frame up, gratis, the bioshelter; and Lillian Leenhouts, solar architect par excellence, who donated the original, sensitive design for the bioshelter;

Jan Christensen, High Wind resident, whose literary acuity and computer savvy made her an ideal partner in the latter years in the production of *Windwatch* (from which I took many excerpts for this book); Louise Mann, whose availability, day and night, for technical assistance during the preparation of the manuscript, was a godsend;

Adelaide Nichols Baker, a dynamic regional (Connecticut) spark plug for all causes dealing with world peace and an observer/consultant to the United Nations for the Women's International League for Peace and Freedom, was a major inspiration and mentor to me. From the time I was a teenager, she fed my growing hunger to become involved with issues and organizations helping to rebuild Europe after World War II. It was through Adelaide (and her family) that I came into contact with the Experiment in International Living, landing my first job in the global arena;

Laird Schaub, good friend and executive secretary of the Federation for Intentional Community, was most helpful in vetting the history of intentional communities through the ages, getting the facts and chronology straight, and clarifying emphases and nuances of the movement in recent decades;

The High Wind Board of Directors, with a revolving constituency drawn both from within the community and from among a galaxy of strong supporters in the broader region. For over thirty years, the board has held us steady and kept us true to our mission;

Bob Pavlik, Marquette University professor and High Wind board member, for always sharing his big heart—with special thanks for creating and analyzing the data from the 2005 High Wind Survey sent to High Wind residents, program leaders, and program participants. Many comments from the survey are included in this book;

Carolyn Kott Washburne, my warm, sensitive, and wise editor, who has shepherded this manuscript through its many incarnations;

Susan Pittelman and Kate Hawley, my savvy production/design team, who worked tirelessly to sharpen and fine-tune my text and to showcase the photographs that together tell the story and capture the spirit of the High Wind adventure exactly as I want to share it.

Table of Contents

Listing of Photo Spreads

Foreword

The purpose of a foreword is to say kind things about a book and the author who wrote it, perhaps giving introductory information or revealing anecdotes that will help the reader have a deeper insight into the material at hand—and to do all this in a few paragraphs.

The first part of this task is easy for me. I've known the author, Lisa Paulson, for many years, and I participated in the beginnings of the High Wind experiment with her and her husband Belden and all the other remarkable people you're about to meet. I have the highest respect and admiration for her, her talents, and the work she did in helping to bring this community into being.

The hard part is saying all I want to say in a brief space. There are so many ways in which I can pay tribute to the people who invested their lives and creativity to make High Wind a reality and to the complex and dynamic person who is Lisa Paulson.

These days, as in the seventies and eighties, there is much talk about the need for intentional community to meet the global challenges of this new century. Living together is seen as a way to reduce our carbon footprint, share resources, provide security for each other, and achieve "resilience," the ability to adapt to changing conditions. Because of my background as a former codirector of the Findhorn Foundation community in northern Scotland, I often get letters from people who say, "I've got the land; what do I do now to start a community?"

The first thing I tell them is that community never starts just with land. It always starts—and grows and is sustained—in the hearts of people.

Now the second thing I can tell them is "Buy and read *An Unconventional Journey*, by Lisa Paulson."

Lisa has written a remarkable book, one that should be a text both for studying the history of the community movement in this country and for anyone thinking of beginning his or her own intentional community. Developing and sustaining such a community is hard work. It has many rewards, but it asks a lot in return. It's no panacea, no easy route. It can easily draw out the best and worst in a person. It can be a heaven one day, a hell the next, and the hellish days can be a lot more frequent for those who are unprepared for the physical, mental, and particularly the emotional and spiritual work such an endeavor can demand.

This is where Lisa's book shines. Findhorn never started out to become a community. There was nothing intentional about it, at least at first. It was for many years just a small group of committed friends sharing a spiritual vision and work that suddenly exploded into being a much larger endeavor, ultimately becoming, for all practical purposes, a small village.

High Wind, on the other hand, began with the intent of being a community (using Findhorn as an inspiration). The vision of community was there from the outset, guiding the choices and plans of its founders. In many ways, this makes it a more useful model than Findhorn for others seeking to do the same thing in the years ahead.

High Wind was also fortunate that from the beginning Lisa had the foresight to document its story through both pictures and words. (I well remember the times I would come up to the community for a visit or to give a workshop or lecture, seeing Lisa with her camera making sure that everything was recorded.) By so doing, she can now give us in this book a no-nonsense, honest, and ultimately an inspiring history about the unconventional journey she, Belden, and all the others took together in service to a vision of planetary wholeness. Furthermore, she places the whole story into the larger social and spiritual context of our time. This makes it more than just the history of one small group of people. It makes it a story relevant to all of us as we move further into the unprecedented challenges, opportunities, and transformations of the twenty-first century.

I happen to agree that community of all kinds is vital for the future of humanity. We need to understand all the myriad ways we are interconnected with each other and with the world around us and work to translate this understanding into practical efforts that develop and sustain wholeness. This is the Hero's Journey of our time, an unconventional but vital, life-affirming journey on which we are all traveling.

This book is the invaluable record of one aspect of this planetary journey into wholeness, recorded and told by a remarkable woman. It is the story of a group of ordinary people who placed their lives on the line to bring something new into being and, in the often difficult process that ensued, discovered that "ordinary" is the new extraordinary.

David Spangler

David Spangler, philosopher and teacher, is the author of many books. His most recent books are *Facing the Future* and *Subtle Worlds: An Explorer's Field Notes*.

Prologue

For the dozen or so years since High Wind ceased to exist as an active "intentional" community—gradually evolving into a looser neighborhood of friends and a foundation seeking out or helping to initiate projects that promote and demonstrate sustainability—I've contemplated writing a history of our experience.

People have said a really juicy, truthful exposé of the shadowy challenges of creating, building, and sustaining such an alternative experiment, encompassing altogether a period of some twenty-five years, could be best-seller material. Along with the dizzying highs, the chronicle would unrelentingly dredge up the moments of frustration, despair, and crankiness; the constant challenge of interpersonal relationships in close quarters; the Herculean difficulty of sitting through endless meetings until we came to consensus about how to proceed. Indeed, for any of us around the world who have dipped into community life, it is always the sticky issues of power, money, and sex that we want to hear about in *other* peoples' communities. This is what we relate to. Here lurk the fascinating tidbits, much more interesting than the bland, sunny, ideological statements that appear in our publicity pieces.

I think, however, I'm not quite ready to "get down to it," naming names and telling all the war stories. I've often said I couldn't safely do this until all our former community members were dead—which would probably be never, as my husband Belden and I, as founders, are nearly a generation older than most of our cohorts.

At the same time, we're aware that a huge body of written experiences that tell our story has been amassed. They need to be collected into some sort of accessible volume, both for historical purposes and to serve as a guide for any new and intrepid adventurers ready to step out of the mainstream to create their own social experiment. Over the years, we did a lot of backing and filling; we were continually bursting with high hopes for various splendid initiatives that fizzled. We discovered through trial and error what worked, what was "authentic," and what all the community members could relate to collectively and could agree to give their energy to.

In 1978, before the community formed, I began writing the first letters to our budding constituency. I shared our thoughts and our vision, keeping them abreast of those exciting initial happenings. Then in 1981, with our embryonic resident group, I launched our newsletter *Windwatch*—typed on

8¹/₂ by 11 inch sheets. *Windwatch* was put together with the help of an artist friend, Patti Neilon, who contributed charming drawings and calligraphy as well as our first sun-and-wind logo. In 1987, Jan Christensen joined the community, bringing sophisticated computer skills; with her help, we switched to a tabloid format we called a "journal," with many more articles by the residents to give varying points of view. Our readership now numbered several thousand High Wind Associates from around Wisconsin as well as across the country and abroad. The residential community had grown to over twenty. Marcia Kjos, one of our residents, was inspired to offer lovely line drawings of prairie plants that picked up the spirit of our relationship to nature, some of which are used in this book. Photos of our land and buildings and people crept onto *Windwatch* pages.

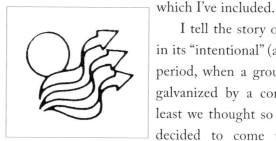
sun-and-wind logo

Because I was the self-appointed "vision-holder," I saw my job as editor not only to become knowledgeable about all aspects of the community, but especially to be able to stand back a bit—almost like a voyeuristic bird perching high in a tree—looking down at the daily rounds with a slightly detached perspective, trying to see how it was all fitting together. I wanted to comment on how the process was working or not working, trying to be as honest as possible in sharing with our public what and how we were doing and where we were heading. At the same time, I have to admit that as one of the founders, I had an enormous emotional stake in what was unfolding, and in my articles, I probably tended to emphasize the highest aspirations and ideals toward which I continually nudged us all. High Wind was "my child" so to speak, and I tended to be protective of her welfare and reputation.

What I draw on here primarily is a token collection of quotes from *Windwatch* and other documents from 1981 through 1992, when High Wind joined with a new endeavor and entity we called Plymouth Institute. The 2005 High Wind Survey that was sent to former High Wind residents, program leaders, and program participants provided a rich sample of comments, many of which I've included.

I tell the story of the community in its "intentional" (and most intense) period, when a group of people was galvanized by a common vision (at least we thought so at the time) and decided to come together to live and play out this particular philosophical idea with very practical implications and imperatives. I continue with some materials that describe what happened after the dissolution of the community aspect within our broader agenda. Throughout, I've selected writings that I believe best depict our evolution and give the flavor of life at High Wind as well as the thinking and trials and activities of its residents.

This book will especially be of interest to those who either lived in the community or who followed its unfolding over the years and who know its spiritual and ecological roots well. But I would like also to reach those not familiar with

High Wind. For this reason, I introduce our history with three chapters that explain how it all began and what the influences were that pushed us in this (some may think "peculiar") direction.

Because I'm the one putting the tale together and had the first glimmerings of what this initiative might be, a bit about how I got to that place may be in order.

After my personal narrative, I trace—in a sketchy, not very methodical, trajectory—the long journey through the history of groups that formed to create "the good life." These were the "intentional communities" that served as reference points and inspiration for contemporary experiments like High Wind. I've shifted the chronology of some of the earlier groups to an appendix to keep the main saga moving easily.

Then comes the story of High Wind itself, from the earliest exciting visions about possibility, through its alternately exhilarating and rocky history, to the gentle winding down of its most active phase. It is not a step-by-step *Sturm und Drang* account but rather an abbreviated portrayal of the highlights (and lowlights) through the years.

I've chosen to convey the character of our life in the community with a collection of photos from the High Wind archives, along with quotations from *Windwatch* and comments from the survey. Together they fill in some of the gaps in my chronicle and bring a sense of immediacy as the residents speak in real time.

I conclude with my and my husband Bel's separate responses to the 2005 High Wind Survey question: "Would you live in community again?"—along with the comments of others. In retrospect, I am surprised at my response.

Lisa Paulson

November 2010

Chapter One

Gale-Force Winds

The most important reason for being in community, the underlying motive for being there, is something one knows on the soul level. Security, companionship, the search for truth, going back to the land, rebellion against society—these are personality needs and none are valid. If the whole of ourselves is engaged, our will, we get into a "sea of knowing," a space of flowing easily....
— *Dorothy Maclean, cofounder of Findhorn Community, from a talk at Lorian-High Wind Seminar, 1983*

My rubber poncho flapped wildly and I bent my head against the driving rain. Navigating over a no-man's-land of sand dunes, weaving across the humps and valleys, and avoiding the prickly spines of scattered gorse bushes, I pressed on to the shore.

I struggled up the last sandy ridge overlooking inky, frothing waters churning onto the shingle below. Balancing in the wind on top of a high dune overlooking the North Sea, I was wrestling with the knowledge that I couldn't go back to the United States to the same life I'd left. I'd just come off three weeks of living in the famed spiritual community called Findhorn, located in a remote corner of Scotland, not far from the Arctic Circle. Working and interacting with three hundred people from every part of the globe, people who clearly were living in close and constant attunement with nature, had turned my life upside down, and at age forty-eight had changed me irrevocably.

A bit of background: The Findhorn community began in 1962 when a middle-aged British couple, Peter and Eileen Caddy, and their Canadian friend, Dorothy Maclean, were directed through meditation to move their ancient trailer to the barren northeast tip of Scotland and to plant a vegetable garden in beach sand.

Following step-by-step instructions, always through meditation, these people (who knew nothing about gardening) achieved such remarkable and improbable results in terms of species and sizes unheard of in those parts that soon hundreds of curious folks from across the world showed up to help and to find out for themselves what this "Factor X" might be—how, somehow, it was possible to communicate with and influence the essence of plants. *The Findhorn Garden*, written by community members in 1968, followed by economist and journalist Paul Hawken's book, *The Magic of Findhorn*, in 1975 had an enormous impact.

Thus the Findhorn community, now called the Findhorn Foundation, was born, which at its height included some three hundred core members. Many more came to settle in its environs in order to partake at varying levels in a panoply of exciting programs and the uniquely inspiring atmosphere.

The community soon perceived its purpose: "to redress the balance between people and nature." It was about humans working in cooperation with nature, recognizing the intrinsic interrelationship and interdependence of all the elements of life on earth.

Those coming to Findhorn from every belief (or nonbelief) system have been drawn to this place of palpable power and energy to follow the practice of being constantly mindful of living in harmony with all they touch, bringing gentleness and caring to every task and interaction.

How all these paths come together is through community members being together in silence. Each person listens to his/her own quiet, inner voice that connects to a wisdom or intelligence transcending individual beliefs or paths, sidestepping personal baggage or bias that might get in the way of coming to clear answers that are in the highest interest of the group.

Soon after understanding how these principles worked in their own lives, in the early 1970s the community created educational programs for the many thousands of visitors who came for varying lengths of time. They came to listen to the ideas and then could put them into practice immediately by pitching into the daily life at Findhorn.

In recent years, this deep respect for nature has translated into projects that address sustainability issues not only within the community itself but also look at environmental crises worldwide. Findhorn's ecovillage is perhaps the strongest and purest model in Britain. The foremost future-oriented thinkers in the world gather regularly in this little experiment in the far North to look squarely at problems and to create innovative solutions.

That day on the dune, all I could do was stand there with rain streaming down my face and shout into the gale: "Okay, I give up. I know I have to take these radical ideas I've been exposed to home to Wisconsin. I know this is what I'm meant to do with my life. But I'll need help, because, hey, I haven't a clue how to begin!"

This culminating moment, this unexpected declaration and commitment, caught even me by surprise. It was also finally clear what my life of rebellion against the status quo, of bumping up against the ceiling of mainstream values and dictates, had been leading up to.

As I listened to my passionate outburst, it felt almost as though I were taking a vow of holy orders. I had stepped behind the walls of a convent, made promises about which I could no longer waffle or renege. I'd jumped into some inexorable river of energy and truth and—Ophelia-like—was allowing myself to float away in the current. Actually, it came as a huge relief. No longer was I standing at a dubious crossroad, teetering between what most of the world expected of me and a whole set of newly discovered realities that was considered downright off-the-wall by the great majority of my contemporaries. It was intimidating.

Findhorn Sand Dunes

It's on these sand dunes, towering above the brooding, crashing North Sea in remote Scotland, that I begin to understand why I was drawn to visit this place called Findhorn. It's the collective vision of its three hundred inhabitants, of people living together in close harmony with each other and nature, that I find so compelling. This is reinforced by my actually experiencing the astonishing energy and clarity of this community as it pursues a path of true sustainability—thirty years before our current recognition of this imperative.

I realize it is this idea and example that I must take back to America.

Findhorn Sand Dune.

It was the fall of 1976, and at Findhorn, I had experienced firsthand community members living together in conscious harmony and in constant communication with some kind of "spirit" or universal intelligence that overlighted the entire natural world—all life. This could be an important ability, I thought, that might even be critical for the continuing existence of our culture and of our world.

I realized that it was what I badly wanted to learn, too. To the challenge of those "voices of the universe" (or whatever I was responding to in the gale-force winds), I could only promise that if they would show me the steps, I was willing to be taken on this peculiar and exciting journey. Through a mysterious series of synchronicities, I had arrived in Scotland, and now, obviously, here was the purpose. The only question was how in the world was I going to communicate such bizarre beliefs and behaviors—such as tuning in to the needs and demands of plants in the garden and vegetables I was peeling in the kitchen, not to mention those of the printing presses in the publishing building—and come across as believable. All of this might seem exceedingly strange to many, and yet I saw this cooperation, this ability to listen, produce astonishing results. Clearly "something" was at work. How, then, to actually put the practices I'd witnessed into concrete form that others could understand and replicate?

Chapter Two

Weaving the Threads Together
My Journey to High Wind

The concept of community in a peace culture implies community on all levels, from integrating the different parts of the self, all the way up to getting the different components comprising our world to work together. Community is an organ of communication and communion, a sharing of viewpoints. It offers an opportunity to step out of ourselves to be part of something larger. Differences and intensity may be an intrinsic part of intentional communities, in order to create at a higher level.

— *David Spangler, Lorian leader, from a High Wind seminar lecture, March 1983*

Before I delve into the birth and unfolding of High Wind, I'd like to share a brief background about my childhood, young adulthood, and early years with Bel—in short, the experiences and beliefs that led me to High Wind.

As with many of us, I've only recently been able to identify recurrent threads that kept popping up in my own disparate collection of life experiences. It took some forty years before I could see how all these seemingly isolated episodes and attitudes connected and made sense. The threads began to overlap and strengthen. Eventually they wove themselves into a recognizable fabric—an insatiable dream that compelled me and others to create High Wind. Though what follows doesn't pertain directly to the story of High Wind, it does offer a close-up glimpse of how one person came to "intentional community." Bear with me, then, as I trace the steps that got me from there to here.

First of all, how did parents who were deeply involved with affairs of the towns they lived in—politics, church, environment-saving initiatives, the arts (with leadership roles)—operating well within the parameters of "normal" conventional values and behavior, produce a daughter like me? One who went out of her way to bend and test the accepted rules and ended up in what many would consider, as did her family, a pretty "far-out" and questionable subculture, almost completely outside the mainstream?

Undoubtedly it had to do with the personality I came to inhabit, or maybe I was just born with a "contrary" gene. Certainly I can trace some reactions back to disagreements with my family. As I went off on my own after college, I was swept up in the disgust a lot of my peers were feeling with the crass culture of business, "getting ahead," and ensuring a secure life. We were on the beginning edge of the rebellion that was soon to explode in the 1960s, and we felt excited at being in the forefront of breaking free from the expected choices of jobs and life paths. The 1950s are often characterized as a decade where people were still trapped in staid, reactionary patterns, but there were definitely pockets of nonconformists who opted out. It was actually a good time to be coming of age.

From a very young age—probably before I was ten—I exhibited an annoying rebel streak; if most people thought and behaved one way, I tended to flaunt the opposite viewpoint. At the same time, I was shy and didn't try to break into the popular cliques in school. I didn't assert myself in college to associate with the visible circle of leadership elites. Growing up, I had a habit of going off alone to sit in forests or at the edge of the remote reservoir in our rural township to soak up the colors of a sunset—and to compulsively scribble poems and essays that captured my feelings and the splendor of those intimate and grand moments in nature.

Another thread contributed to this distancing from the dominant kid culture. I grew up with parents who were intellectually curious and driven by a strong sense of social justice. This broadened to include interest in cultural diversity and involvement in world affairs. These were values I could finally agree with (especially as World War II was breaking out). A close family friend, a delegate to the United Nations, was pivotal in pushing our entire family to work on peace initiatives. Our home in Weston, Connecticut, close to New York City, was often filled with exotic representatives from the U.N. "International understanding" was a major

goal, and it was exciting to be exposed to people and ideas from around the globe. I became sensitive to issues that both connected and divided nationalities.

It was probably this attraction to other cultures that led me to my first communal experience. Fresh out of college, I landed a job in the rural hills of Vermont with a pioneering organization, the Experiment in International Living. Residing and working in a venerable farmhouse, the close-knit staff was comprised of about a dozen young people from Germany, France, Austria, and Holland as well as the United States. We arranged for high school and college-age students to live with small town families in countries all across the globe.

In off hours, we cooked and laughed together, climbed mountains, skate-sailed with sheets on our pond at midnight, boiled up cauldrons of a wicked barberry liqueur in the mailroom, participated in a community theater production, and dug each other out of ditches in mud season. When the maple sap was running, everybody took time out to collect the buckets with a team of horses and keep the fires going in the sugarhouse. Ours was a rich, collective social life, and there was nothing remotely resembling the usual dating scene.

After a summer leading an Experiment group to southern France, which included camping and climbing in the Alps, my feet were wet and my appetite whetted, and I hungered for a longer stay abroad. It was this international focus that drew me back to Europe again and again, to visit and then to live for several years, nurturing the seeds of my early curiosity and concern about the world. Along with many others in that postwar era, I felt the

Lisa Leads a Student Group to France

My first adventure abroad takes me to southern France in 1951. Co-leading a group of twelve college students for the Vermont-based Experiment in International Living, the participants and I are each housed with a different French family.

We spend a month totally immersed in the local village life of our hosts. The next month we invite our French "sisters" and "brothers" to join us in biking from sea level into the high Alps where we rock climb and traverse glaciers.

Hiking above timberline in the French Alps.

Lisa sailing to France on the student ship *Nelly*, leading a group for the Experiment in International Living, 1951.

significance of connecting deeply with people everywhere, of discovering commonalities and bridging surface differences.

After two years with the Experiment program, I decided to go back to Europe on my own to immerse myself in work that could be genuinely useful. This was 1952, and I'd seen the devastation still evident in Europe after the war and so, armed with a pre-Peace-Corps-type idealism, I landed in France. With backpack and a friend, I wandered through several countries, ending up, almost penniless, in Rome. There I heard about a "crazy American," one Belden Paulson, doing relief work in the bombed-out ruins of Naples. My ears pricked up because I recognized the name as an Oberlin classmate, though we'd never met.

That same day, my friend Ann Louise Coffin (Annie) and I took a train south and in the middle of the night, eventually found our way to Bel's obscure, rusty gate in the midst of the rubble. Somewhat astonished, he kindly took us in and the next day hired me to work at the center he was running. It was called Casa Mia—My Home. This became my next "community" experience. I learned street Italian in a hurry so as to be able to communicate with this team of fiercely dedicated Neapolitans and work with them among the five hundred homeless who came daily for activities at Casa Mia. I also went out alone to assess needs in the bleak caves where the destitute and forgotten were barely existing.

Bel was a kindred rebel, up for tilting colossal windmills at any status-quo situation, daring to launch "impossible" projects when others only whined. Over the course of the year, our relationship ripened. (Proximity is a wonderful stimulus!) In fall, we returned to the States, and we got married in 1954. We spent the next three years at the University of Chicago while Bel completed coursework for his PhD. In 1956, when our son Eric was just two weeks old, we were surprised by a visit from Don Murray, the conscientious objector volunteer who had replaced Bel at Casa Mia and was now a well-known film actor. Don had always said if he had any success as an actor, he would use his resources to help the refugees he (and we) had assisted in Naples. These were Iron Curtain escapees from communist regimes who had landed in Italy but were considered "hardcore" (rejected for immigration by all the countries they applied to)—and probably destined to live out their lives in barbed wire camps. Don told us he had money in his pocket from playing in the movie *Bus Stop* opposite Marilyn Monroe and was ready to try to get some refugees out of the camps. Were we ready, too?

At first, we said no; how could we walk out on the planned doctoral schedule? Finally, Bel agreed to take time out for a short exploratory trip to Europe with Don, just to look at possibilities. But, inevitably, as they talked to officials up and down Italy, they both became so inspired by the challenge that Bel (and I) soon knew we were going back to anchor whatever project evolved. The dissertation would be put on hold.

The place we selected to resettle refugees was the island of Sardinia off Italy's west coast. This was urged on us by Italian officials who promised significant subsidies. The island was

Lisa Meets Bel in Naples

In 1952, I feel an urgency to leave my position with the Experiment in International Living to return to Europe on my own. Having glimpsed a bit of the appalling destruction from World War II, I hope to plug in somewhere to help.

Improbably, a white Russian prince running the World Council of Churches in Rome suggests a project in Naples. I'm curious, because it is headed by a former Oberlin College classmate, Belden Paulson, whose name I recognize. I had never met this Belden Paulson, but, somewhat miraculously, find him amidst the bombed-out wreckage of Naples. He promptly takes me on as a volunteer at Casa Mia, the first social settlement center in Italy. After nearly a year of working with five hundred homeless who come to the center for programs and meals—and having fallen in love—Bel and I return to the States and marry.

Lisa and Bel take a break in Sorrento from their work stint in bombed-out Naples, 1953.

Lisa and Bel return to Italy to resettle Iron Curtain refugees in Sardinia, 1957.

An Unconventional Journey

underpopulated and now ripe for development after years of a devastating plague of malaria that was finally eliminated. So in fall 1957, Bel, Eric, and I, with a couple of peace church (pacifist) volunteers, found ourselves almost the only Americans on this still largely preindustrial island. Don and his wife, actress Hope Lange, stayed behind in California to raise funds for the project.

Gradually we brought Yugoslavs, Hungarians, Albanians, Czechs, and even Spaniards to Sardinia, together creating the Homeless European Land Program (HELP). We cleared cactus off the 135 acres HELP had bought and brought in irrigation. Small industries were set up: truck farming, orange groves, a chicken business, concrete-block making. With myriad needs and challenges, this very diverse collection of folks became another community of sorts—distinct from, yet functioning within the context of the local Sardinian village culture. Bel and I began to get valuable practice in the decision-making process and sorting out thorny interpersonal relationships as well as in creating a group economic base—major challenges we were to be faced with later at High Wind.

Because the United Nations was partially supporting the refugee camps in Italy, the U.N. High Commissioner for Refugees in Geneva became very interested in our model for resettling refugees within Italy. They were especially interested because our experiment defied the conventional wisdom of authorities who said these refugees could not be rehabilitated; they were doomed to life in the camps.

After two years in Sardinia, Bel was asked to join the staff of the U.N. in Rome, with the mission of mounting a plan to clear refugees from the camps on a broad scale. We spent the next couple of years in Rome, living in a totally different milieu. For me, it felt like coming full circle, returning to the city where eight years before I'd been reduced to sitting on curbs when I was faint from hunger. This time, though, I was part of a rich cosmopolitan environment of journalists, novelists, film people, diplomats, and entrepreneurs of many nationalities, again something of a distinct and self-contained community. And here our second son, Steve, was born.

The next events to contribute to the convergence of my threads of nonconformity, gravitation to community, and connecting with divergent strands of humanity came some five years later when, in 1967, our family of four went to live for a year in Northeast Brazil. When we had returned to the United States after two years in Rome, I'd experienced real culture shock, essentially becoming a suburban housewife. After our peripatetic, cosmopolitan, if wildly unstable, life abroad, I felt suddenly stifled, without a "mission." I'd been spoiled by life on the front lines and now faced a real identity crisis. In 1962, we settled in Milwaukee where Bel, after having taken a year at the University of Chicago to complete his dissertation about a communist village near Rome, had landed a job teaching at the Milwaukee campus of the University of Wisconsin.

When a grant for research in Brazil came up, all four of us leaped at the chance to escape to what promised to be another cutting-edge adventure. Fortaleza, a city on the northeast coast, just south of the equator, offered yet again a very different cultural experience. We were dropped into an expatriate group of American agricultural resource advisors. In addition, Bel had to wing it with the local university where he was based with his Brazilian student research team, as well as joust with the regional power structure. (He was trying to find out why the political system in the Northeast couldn't do more to alleviate the starvation and poverty in this drought-prone area—why it didn't allow the constructed reservoirs to be used for irrigation and food production—and the local mayors had a tendency to hold their cards close to the vest.)

Out of curiosity, in addition to trying to run a fairly primitive household (in Portuguese) and entertain visiting family and academics, and play cello in the city orchestra, I opened myself up to participating in the rituals and beliefs of a couple of native religious practices in Fortaleza: Macumba (voodoo) and Spiritism. For much of my life, I'd had intimations of a mysterious dimension existing below the radar of our own largely scientific, skeptical society. Sometimes it surfaced as conventional faith, but there was the occasional dip into quirky mysticism. Here in Northeast Brazil, where three cultures have come together—Portuguese and African descendants, along with indigenous Indians—there is, even among the more educated, a conviction that the veil separating this world from the next is very thin. I definitely sensed that because this belief was so prevalent, the spirit world *was* indeed closer than at home, and most people performed little superstitious rituals "just in case."

My personal experience was complex and frightening, involving a sudden, intractable illness.

I found I was almost entirely paralyzed physically, had a continual, searing headache, and also thought I was losing my mind. I was terrified that I'd never get out of Brazil alive. My condition was picked up by a psychic medium who regularly visited our household helper in our garden. He was sure it was caused by an evil eye spell, that it had originated in a Macumba session I'd attended. These rituals melded the worship of African deities and Catholic saints, and would respond, I was told, only to an exorcism ceremony with Spiritist mediums. (This sect was imported in the nineteenth century from France.) The exorcism did work, incidentally, or *something* cured me, almost on the spot. All this was anthropologically interesting, and, in retrospect, even humorous, but definitely not so at the time!

On our return to Wisconsin, my awareness of otherworldly or unconventional sources of power was further fueled by a course in self-hypnosis, or mental imaging, that we took as a family. The practical results for each one of us were so compelling that I jumped in to work with the instructor to develop a school for teaching altered states of consciousness (Psy-Bionics). We found that at a subconscious level, one apparently could direct outcomes for health and other life conditions by believing in and imagining specific goals while in a deeply relaxed state. We also saw how these techniques might be accessing some of those supernatural dimensions I'd encountered in Brazil.

As our classes mushroomed, we organized several national conferences at the University of Wisconsin in Milwaukee. We brought in leaders in paranormal research from across the country, as well as psychologists and other noted and credible investigators of this little-understood field. People were curious, the response enormous. I should add that becoming involved with Psy-Bionics finally dissolved the shyness and insecurity I'd carried around for years. Soon not only was I writing publicity materials, but I was also giving talks, teaching classes, and counseling individuals. I'd found my own voice, my identity, and saw this work as one of several "serial passions" that have completely taken over my life through the years. (Music and painting were others.)

Along the way, in the course of these lectures (it was 1973), I kept hearing very reputable scientists referring to what they said was "the most important spiritual experiment in the world." They were referring to the Findhorn community in Scotland. I listened, intrigued by wild stories of how oversized and unusual plants were being grown in beach sand not far from the Arctic Circle. What made this possible was step-by-step instruction received in meditation by the founders of this group. It seemed that direct communication was established with the patterning life force in each species of plant. The response had been so amazing that, as word got out, some three hundred people from all over the world had converged on this desolate corner of northeast Scotland to practice living in this kind of conscious cooperation with nature.

Quickly I boned up on Findhorn, read the few books that had been published, and realized I simply had to go there—by myself. This was an essential next step I needed to take. It was a spiritual quest. It was also a quest to clarify (and solidify) my personal identity and life purpose.

In the fall of 1976, I flew off to Scotland. Beyond all the stories of mystical happenings, what I actually experienced far exceeded my expectations. In the three weeks I lived and worked in the community and attended Findhorn's prestigious annual international conference, I began to see in clearer perspective old personal habits and constructs, and for the first time could actually step away from them. Letting go of my usual chewing over baggage from the past and meticulously planning for the future, I experienced the feeling of stepping into a river of energy and letting myself be swept along in that present moment—trusting to "spirit," trusting that whatever the outcome, it would be the right one.

Over and over there were synchronistic occurrences. For instance, the person I wanted to meet (there were six hundred present at this world gathering) would sit down next to me at lunch. This was a switch from fixing goals, as we had practiced at Psy-Bionics; I began to see that perhaps there were intelligences at work that knew better than I (at a conscious level anyway) what needed to happen, better than I might "program" on my own. What I was now learning went a step beyond Psy-Bionics. It meant articulating a problem, a situation, options—releasing the question or request and proceeding with absolute trust in the outcome. Both paths, though, depended on the ability to work with inner promptings or guidance.

The conference speakers at Findhorn were some of the leading thinkers and practitioners in the

Lisa's First Visit to Findhorn

In 1976, I embark on what begins as a personal quest. Eventually this becomes a mission of drawing together hungry seekers from around the American Midwest to embrace, and then try to live out, a new cultural paradigm—a different way of seeing and being in the world. I land at Findhorn, the renowned spiritual "intentional community" in the northeast corner of Scotland. For three heady weeks, I live and work along with Findhorn's multiethnic members in their gardens, kitchens, printing shop, and construction operations. I also sit in on sessions of a prestigious, annual international conference, not only hearing about ideas that are radically prescient, but also picking up a visceral sense of being with people who are in touch with a very unusual source of wisdom and power and gentleness.

Findhorn Bay, harbor for the ancient fishing village of Findhorn, adjoins the Findhorn community caravan park.

Lisa at the gorge at Randolph's Leap, near Findhorn, 1976.

Universal Hall, Findhorn's conference center, built by the community and many visitors over several years.

world. They talked about a global environmental/resource crisis, which was rare in the 1970s, and crises on many other fronts as well (economic, with deepening gaps between the haves and have-nots; inadequacies on educational fronts). Buckminster Fuller (American architect and inventor who designed the geodesic dome) was quoted: "We're making the mistake of living off our *principal* (non-renewable resources) when we should be living on the *interest* (renewable energy)."

At Findhorn, all this had translated into people taking these challenges seriously and beginning to establish a balance between human beings and nature. It meant honoring a vision of stepping together on a path of commitment to birth and model a new "planetary culture," of sharing resources, of growing and preparing food cooperatively, of pooling equipment and machinery, of sharing walls, of building "green." Thus, Findhorn was becoming what they called a "center of light," beginning to demonstrate how to live in a more healthy, fulfilling, and sustainable way into the long-term future.

Believing that "work is love in action," people were joining them from nearly every country to live in and build this cradle for "intentional communities." I found myself remembering the impulse from my early twenties to bridge cultural gaps, and I resonated deeply with this demonstration of diverse people connecting to pursue an ideal together. Here it was a collective spiritual quest where some mystical thread seemed to weave through that human tapestry of individuals attracted by the possibility of communicating and interacting directly with nature, with the earth.

Findhorn was also creating educational programs so that thousands more could come for shorter periods to experience a different and eminently graceful way of life. It was looking up at the sky and seeing the broad sweep of a vision while keeping one's feet planted firmly on the ground of hard work. It meant living with integrity and honesty in relationships with others and seeing sacredness and beauty in the ordinary. It meant approaching both grand and menial jobs with equal enthusiasm, and caring meticulously for the materials and tools one works with. Any line between work and play vanished, because everything one did was seen as important and exhilarating. This is what I experienced during the three weeks I was there, letting go of old patterns and opening up to entirely new modes of thinking and being.

And so I found myself balancing in the wind on top of a sand dune overlooking the North Sea, wrestling with the knowledge that I couldn't go back to the United States to the same life that I'd left only three weeks before.

And, as when something is right, I *was* shown, step by step. It turned out that back home there was a great hunger for the story of Findhorn, and I was drafted to give many slide talks around our region.

Shortly after I got back, we experienced another uncanny example of synchronicity. The phone rang and a voice said, "This is Angelynn Brown. Do you remember that we met at Findhorn? I had a dream last week that I was to leave the community immediately and move to Milwaukee to do spiritual work with you."

(I recalled that when I had heard there was a Findhorn member from my adopted hometown, Milwaukee, I had looked her up. She was busily running the community kitchen, and we chatted just briefly.) Very soon after the call, Angelynn showed up on our doorstep and lived with us for the next several years. She played a pivotal role in helping me to interpret Findhorn and its philosophy. Together we organized study groups and gave talks around the region. We tapped her artistic talents to create a stunning poster announcing our first major public event.

In June 1977, Bel and I brought Findhorn's founders, Peter and Eileen Caddy, to speak at the University of Wisconsin-Milwaukee, and they ignited a fire under twelve hundred people at this groundbreaking event. (By now Bel was enthusiastically on board with these concepts and gradually shifted the focus of his university department to "futures studies.") The Lorian group, spearheaded by David Spangler and Milenko Matanovic, both of whom had been influential in articulating Findhorn's purposes in its early years, arrived to teach academic courses with us for the next six years.

a slide lecture by
Peter and Eileen Caddy
Co-founders of findhorn

findhorn is a new age community-an extraordinary experiment of man and nature in co-operation. Thousands have been drawn to this barren peninsula in Northern Scotland by miracle stories of gigantic vegetables and roses blooming in the snow. With 300 slides the Caddys will tell how an awareness of the divinity within, and the interconnectedness of all life — with a grounding in physical work — first produced the legendary garden, and now is growing a new breed of people — people who move intuitively and have learned that with faith and love they can tap into little known and unlimited sources of energy. Findhorn's vision is the creation of a new planetary culture, through the transformation of human consciousness.

Thursday June 30 8 p.m.
UWM-Union, Wisconsin Room
$3.00 ~ students $2.00

Sponsored by
Center for Urban Community Development, UW-Extension
Division of Urban Outreach, UWM and UW-Extension
School of Fine Arts

for information call 332-9503 or 224-4143

They held our hands as we launched the High Wind Association, a venture dedicated both to creating models of renewable energy and seeing this partnership with nature as our overlighting spiritual path. We were equally drawn to the experiments of John Todd's New Alchemy Institute (the pioneering group in the United States working with renewable energy and permaculture, which we visited at their sites in Cape Cod and on Prince Edward Island in Canada) and to Findhorn's global breadth and relationship with spirit. Both were setting early examples that became the foundation for the current imperative for a sustainable world.

So the threads that early on in my life seemed mostly unconnected and ephemeral finally came together to form a cohesive vision, a progression of experiences, and a configuration of convictions that literally pushed me into the adventure that was High Wind.

Chapter Three

The Contemporary Community Movement

What kind of bridges can or must be built to the main cultural stream? The most important question I feel we have to address is whether these intentional communities are signposts to an aspect of the future or simply a manifestation of inevitable disorders and adjustments brought about by the changing industrial order. Are they reactive or proactive, aberrations or evolutionary social mutations? We may be convinced of the latter, but it behooves us to make a point in the language and with arguments that not only the public but also decision-makers can recognize and appreciate as being relevant to their problems. We must recognize that this is a bridging exercise and not a gathering of the converted. We must, if need be, craft a new manner of relating that will allow society to value these centers for their full potential.

— Francois Duquesne, Findhorn leader, at a brainstorming series organized around the idea of an alternative think tank in Wisconsin, February 1986

Many prior movements were building blocks in the creation of the High Wind experiment—from the Essenes in Palestine in the second century B.C.E., to the Amana Colony in Iowa in the mid-1800s, to Twin Oaks in Virginia, which is going strong today.

I think it would be helpful (and interesting) to provide some background about what influenced the creation of High Wind. (In order not to interrupt the focus of my High Wind narrative, I've put a brief description of the earlier community movements into Appendix Two, "The Perennial Quest for 'The Good Life.'" I invite you to read this overview of significant historical precedents to High Wind.)

By the mid-twentieth century, the United States was a country poised on an edge, ready to explode out of a lot of tamped-down emotions. It was the stillness before the deluge.

We (along the East Coast, anyway) felt held down under a mask of propriety and decorum symbolized by the de rigueur calling cards (calling cards!) our mothers carried in the 1940s and early 1950s, by the white gloves we wore, and by the discrete little veils on our pillbox hats covering our eyes (all of which were soon to be tossed away). We ached under an unarticulated feeling of repression. We thirsted for the kind of freedom where we could connect with primal instincts allowing us to defy all that enveloped our static world, kept so neatly in place in our segment of society.

Blacks and women in their oppressive strait-jackets had begun to seethe and smolder. We (mainly the young people of the "privileged classes") grasped at the righteous anger we reveled in and were eager to help break that yoke. First, we had been paralyzed into frightened silence by the McCarthy-era witch hunt, then we were burned by the insanity and futility of the Vietnam War, then we were appalled and outraged by the violence coming to light in the South. We who were sufficiently well fed to be able to indulge in philosophizing and dreaming about a life that was altogether different—a luxury beyond the grasp or imagination of those in survival mode—came thundering and blundering into the 1960s.

The lid flew off; some of us marched in Alabama, some left comfortable suburban homes to band together in California and then spread out across the country in earnest little urban and rural groupings. A new underground culture was born that set itself up in juxtaposition to and in defiance of what we saw as the complacent, insidious, evil norms of the mainstream.

The mid-twentieth century was about to claim its place among the estimable parade of communal experiments through the ages.

THE DILEMMA

We often hear people say one of the compelling needs today is for a greater sense of purpose and meaning in our lives. There's a longing to break out of what has become a fairly narrow, self-serving culture, too often emphasizing petty, partisan, materialistic goals. From the beginning, this country had visions of the larger common good: a unified nation, participatory democracy, a free society, equal opportunity, elimination of war, protection from material want. None of these has been fully embodied, and even though such aspirations have inspired individual lives, we're being affected by circumstances that threaten to block

many of our dreams and certainly threaten the general culture.

Just in the last few decades we've come to realize we live in a truly interdependent global community where the future consequences of our present actions are taking on great importance. We've become not just Americans but citizens of the planet. Consider some recent environmental crises: the nuclear accident at Chernobyl, the build-up of CO_2 that creates global warming, the thinning of the ozone layer that protects us from ultra-violet radiation (due to use of petrochemicals), acid rain, loss of topsoil, clear-cutting of trees that let the earth breathe. We see clearly that there's no place left to hide. One problem is that we're living in a global political community and a global economy, but we're still saddled with a maze of parochial nation states.

When a civilization on a static plateau is challenged by the natural or social environment, it has to respond in some way. The success of the response determines whether there will be a new period of growth or one of disintegration leading to collapse. We need creativity, flexibility, and prophetic minorities. When social structures and behavior patterns become rigid and conformist, and when the dominant institutions hang onto prerogatives without opening the culture to new forces and ideas, then creative change is blocked.

No civilization can take its survival for granted. Often there's a feeling we must be confronted with a true crisis on all fronts, an absolute breakdown of society, before people are ready to look at alternatives and make the quantum leap in numbers sufficient to shift our basic paradigms and effect fundamental change.

The United States, with a fraction of the world's population, consumes a huge, disproportionate percentage of the world's goods—as well as a high percentage of its fossil fuels and other nonrenewable resources. Have-not countries have begun to show muscle in protesting this gross imbalance. Already this has resulted in political insecurity around the world: arms races, terrorism, the threat of nuclear blackmail, new wars. Where once America was welcomed as the model, the savior of the world, more recently we're the resented, distrusted, and even detested pariah.

Despite our galloping scientific advances, the limits of resources and thus of production and growth are becoming inevitable. Unless we continue to bury our heads in the sand, clearly we will come to a point where we realize Americans will have less money and fewer goods, and we'll have to learn to live on less.

With a few broad strokes, I'll pinpoint some of the more contemporary parallel initiatives worldwide that became significant historical precedents. I'm not trying to be historically perfect or exact in my descriptions, but I am giving a general picture of the way these ideals unfolded and played out over time.

Others may certainly offer different assessments of the flavors of the specific decades over the past forty-odd years—what the 1960s, 1970s, and 1980s were all about. I will describe the conditions in these years as I've seen them—the cultural and physical environment that made our own efforts to create High Wind seem imperative. This is my own sense, my own experience of these eras, and they are unapologetically personal.

THE COMMUNITY MOVEMENT BLOSSOMS IN THE MID-TWENTIETH CENTURY

The mid-twentieth century seemed to mark a unique turning point; there hadn't been such a conspicuous shifting since the Middle Ages. In many circles, particle science was no longer accepted as gospel. Human consciousness and intuitive knowing began to be cautiously accepted as causality, as valid as empirical test tube science. When Bel and I visited China in 1989, we conferred with eminent scientists who said it has actually been downhill since Newton's reductionist pronouncements; the Chinese spoke easily of subjects American scholars might believe too far out to consider. They said, for example, that it's obvious we came from and will go on to inhabit other planets.

In response to the crises mentioned earlier and to new questioning of pure science as the answer to everything, a small, leaderless minority began to form, an underground believing that a fundamental change of society was necessary, starting with a basic shift in attitudes and paradigms. In the 1960s, this manifested as protest against the Vietnam War—against what the prevailing society espoused or accepted. It was not, at first, an effort to create a better world, but was, most conspicuously, young people (often from privileged families) who were opting out of the mainstream. Then the purpose of some of them changed as they looked at the wider picture, and they sought to rip open the fabric of what they saw as an ossified society. They wanted to expose hypocrisies in the political and social scene: the injustices, inequities, prejudices. Much that was rigid and unspoken was finally out in the open and smashed, hopefully, they thought, forever. This decade marked the beginning of the peace movement, feminism, and the push for civil rights.

Early on there was little critical discernment as to who was accepted into the living arrangements (often "crash pads") of these groups. The new freedom was celebrated with open rebellion against families and the flaunting of indiscriminate sex and recreational drugs. These enclaves were too unstable and un-thought-out to last, but they were important in starting to unglue the immobility of society. Then, drawing in freer thinkers of all ages, they began to launch real political change, breaking up bourgeois patterns and racism. We saw cities blowing up over civil rights, including the incendiary uprising in Watts; angry demonstrations against the Vietnam War; aspirants to high political office, such as Eugene McCarthy and George McGovern, who challenged the system and attracted enormous followings; chaos and ferment in the big universities across the country, such as Berkeley, UW-Madison, and Columbia.

Since that time, some of those concerned with the cultural malaise have been coming together in "intentional communities." These are defined, as I implied earlier, as groups sharing particular values and goals who agree to live together and try to live these values in daily life. This, they feel, will ultimately change the culture. These people know they're not perfect and they don't have all the answers, but they have committed to taking the step of walking this path.

The forerunner of some of the communities that took root in the 1970s and 1980s in the U.S. (and around the world) began with Findhorn in Scotland in 1962. My visit there was described in the preceding chapter. In the first wave of well-established American communities that are still going strong today is Twin Oaks in Virginia. Designed around the behaviorist theories of B.F. Skinner in 1967, it spurred several other egalitarian offshoots around the country.

The Farm, in Tennessee, was founded by Stephen Gaskin, who led a caravan of hippies east from California in 1970. A bit later, among a flurry of experimental enclaves, came Sirius near Amherst, Massachusetts, in 1978, started by ex-Findhornians, and then High Wind. In time, most of these became practicing ecovillages—a community of people demonstrating a sensitivity to conservation, energy efficiency, and preservation of natural resources and an awareness of their relationship to the larger world. These are just a few examples that we happen to know well; there were hundreds of others, including those in the North

> I see High Wind and initiatives like it contributing to a better world in the future because they are laboratories testing new ideas—they're able to do something small on behalf of large ideas; they're willing to go through difficult and cumbersome processes; they can give shape to difficult-to-understand ideas; they share insights with others and connect with society.
> — *Milenko Matanovic, Lorian leader, 2005 High Wind Survey*

American umbrella groups, Fellowship for Intentional Community and the income-sharing Federation of Egalitarian Communities.

Some of these intentional communities have been called "New Age," a term that had a good deal of purity of intent in those early days but now is shunned by many groups that may fall into that category. The phrase has been so pilloried and ridiculed, especially by the media (and has been prostituted by fringe elements in the ranks of some communities themselves) that members go out of their way to explain themselves in other ways. David Spangler, a philosopher who lived at Findhorn and is considered to be one of the shapers of the modern New Age movement, defined it as "both an objective shift of energy and consciousness that humanity is going through at the moment and, more importantly, a metaphor or a reminder of our ability to be creatively original and innovative, able to think outside the historical box, particularly in a manner that opens us to the presence of love and possibility and the creation of wholeness."

The twentieth-century initiatives had a flavor different from those mid-nineteenth century utopian communities. The experimental groups of the 1800s didn't change the basic course of society, and the outside systems and values continued much as before—although there were significant contributions, such as kindergartens and public libraries. Now the mainstream is widely perceived as being in deep trouble. Also, currently the United States is more clearly connected to the rest of the world with, for example, nuclear and environmental threats to all, as well as widespread terrorist attacks. So by the 1980s, some of the groups were not dropping out but were intent on building a new society, one that might even help figure out how to save the human race. The majority of the contemporary communities in this country, though, have been primarily focused on creating a good life for their own members.

Because the groups today are usually structured with shared leadership, they're generally distinct from more authoritarian enclaves, a few of which also sprang up at the same time. I've often heard the warning: if any one person says his or her way is the *only* way, the *right* way—run! At the same time, however, there is need for members to surrender to each other to see what emerges, surrender themselves to a collective image as it becomes apparent. This can only happen in a group context.

I should say here that Laird Schaub, a good friend and executive secretary of the Federation for Intentional Community, has been invaluable in vetting my information—helping with the chronology of the community lineage, pointing out nuances I missed, getting my historical facts straight. He wanted to be sure I noted a significant difference between the alternative groups before World War II and those that came after: that a much larger percentage of the communities today are secular (that is, a spiritual path is not a condition of membership).

At the same time, I need to say that we at High Wind do partially come out of the spiritually grounded Findhorn tradition, but, like that community, High Wind and others we know haven't pushed or insisted on any particular spiritual path or ritual as did the earlier religious groups. In fact, we never asked what our members believed or if they believed anything at all. We preferred to talk about being a "community of consciousness," not going too far beyond saying we were about taking care of the earth and each other. Whatever anyone felt or believed came out of some aspect of this.

The new openness in this time led to a hunger to go deeper on psychological levels, and it began to be acceptable to talk of and express feelings. Many paths and techniques sprang up in the 1970s. Some of these practices took people to techniques for self-actualization and conflict resolution and also into exploration of paranormal or mystical levels of consciousness. I plunged into est, *I'm OK–You're OK*, bioenergentics, *Games People Play*, gestalt, Transactional Analysis, and the Enneagram.

No longer were people content to be sheep, stumbling like sleepwalkers through the paces dictated by a frenetic culture driven by consumerism and one-upmanship. Some got off that train, realizing there was something else more important, much finer. They began to change personal paradigms, the way they looked at the world. They trusted their own instincts more, weren't afraid to "follow their bliss," as Joseph Campbell urged. They identified what they felt passionate about and went for it. In the 1970s and into the 1980s (the "Me decade"), people (probably more women) said to themselves, "It's my turn" and went in search of new directions, new agendas. Self-help and awareness then often morphed into a drive to help others, to be of service to the larger whole.

So what were the communities of the 1980s like? For one thing, there were fewer of them; not as many people chose to live collectively, and some

folks who had joined enthusiastically were giving up and returning to the mainstream—though taking with them new skills and sensitivities. The 1980s communities were different from those of the 1960s and 1970s, partly, perhaps, out of reaction. Some of them consolidated three distinct movements from the '70s: spiritual (or consciousness), human potential, and ecological, realizing that we can't separate these as we look at each other and inhabit the planet.

At Findhorn in 1982, as different configurations were discussed, I heard the definition of a "planetary village": "A community living its own life as if the planet mattered, developing visionary approaches to ecology, horticulture, governance, education, personal growth, group dynamics, business, the arts." How, you may ask, is this different from an intentional community? Many intentional communities are indeed also planetary villages, fitting into the above description. Some, though, have opted to remain more closed, their residents intent primarily on creating a fulfilling life for their own enclave—the homesteading model. There are also groups considering themselves planetary villages whose members are joined by a shared intent of world service, education, and outreach. They may live more independently, but their land is often held jointly, with common areas or land cooperatives and/or land trusts. Planetary villages are less parochial than traditional mainstream villages.

Because *both* intentional communities and the new villages have more internal cooperation and more independence from larger systems, they may be the best way to weather current and looming crises in order to create a "humane, sustainable culture." Their method is to encourage change from the inside out, not top down—by personal example, not through broad legislation and institutions. It is also recognized in intentional community circles that there are two major kinds of communities, those embracing a collective wisdom and those surrendering to the wisdom of a living avatar. High Wind was a group that favored the former and frowned on the latter.

Intentional communities are seen as a chance to mesh individual dreams in the daily round with others who share the same values and are working co-creatively with nature and spirit. People are (ideally) relating to each other with more gentleness and heart. There is intuitive decision-making and action rather than relying on the purely analytical approach. Time is spent getting in touch with and trusting the deep-est part of the self. The community movement can demonstrate commitment to nonviolence, cooperative, simple living, and respect for the earth—all of which may be the only way our species can continue on the planet.

Such alternative groups believe in taking the long view of the future, recalling the historical way of the Iroquois Indians who made decisions based on what would be good for the next seven generations. Decisions were made not only for one's immediate community but for the human race and all of life on earth. It is felt now that we can no longer afford to live in ways that ignore the inter-connectedness of people and nature and survive.

All these lofty goals, if realized, would produce a more perfect society. I need to stress at this point, however, that hard as groups might try, when they actually start living together, the reality on the ground seldom matches the glowing rhetoric that attracts hungry seekers like a magnet. The business of existing and working together in close-knit enclaves is very tough, and problems of interpersonal relationships often trump all the other challenges of attempting to create a new societal model. So if even only *some* of the stated objectives are achieved, the groups may be commended for taking big risks and contributing valuable examples that at least may point the way to "the possible."

> The values of community and environmental sustainability that High Wind championed have never lost their power and salience. If there was a "deficiency," it was not in the project of High Wind itself but in the larger vision and spiritual movement that High Wind was a part of. That's where the limitations came from. Put simply, we didn't have a plan for getting the rest of the world to create realities that looked like ours.
>
> — *Judith Pintar, High Wind program participant, 2005 High Wind Survey*

PHILOSOPHICAL AND SPIRITUAL IDEAS UNDERPINNING THE NEW GROUPINGS

What is the new vision? For two hundred years, most of the Western world has functioned with the reductionist way of thinking. Briefly, reductionism posits that the material world is a mosaic of an infinite number of separate pieces assembled into an enormous machine. The conduct of science is prone to reductionism, all the more because of the resulting successes in engineering and physical progress, such as being able to send probes to other planets; we now have the mathematics and expertise to do this. It's easy to conclude, "The only thing going on here is . . . ." It was this approach that shaped the Industrial Revolution. Or was it the Industrial Revolution that changed our thinking?

In any case, this mindset has also kept us from exploring a complementary approach: whole-systems thinking. A good number of the new scientists, especially physicists and biologists, are beginning to see that the world is actually an indivisible whole where all the parts, including each of us, are in dynamic relationship.

This is the "Gaian perspective." (Gaia was the Earth goddess of the Greeks.) The premise is that the Earth itself is a living, sentient being where all life is interconnected by what might be thought of as a divine spark. It's the idea that a sneeze in the United States may be felt in India; this has sometimes been called "the butterfly effect," because it is believed that a butterfly's wings flapping in China may trigger a change in a large air mass somewhere else—calling in chaos theory, where cause and effect are more difficult to predict.

Chaos theory posits that apparently disordered phenomena actually have an underlying order. There are systems whose states evolve over time and are highly sensitive to minute effects, such as the flapping of the butterfly's wings. Large systems are complex, making them hard to predict,

> As a macrocosm of the interpersonal relationship, the community lives and breathes as a single unit. Its success depends on commitment to trust, even in times of ambiguity.
>
> — *Etienne (Steve) Schuh, High Wind resident, from a paper for Three-Community Seminar, 1984*

and the resulting randomness may be replaced by an amazing (if fleeting) kind of order.

There's also the belief that we don't live *on* the earth, but *within* Gaia. We're really all one species in a planet-wide scheme. There's not necessarily a purpose but a *sense* of purpose that's fully automatic, where many species play a part. Along with our power of reason, we humans must also use imagination and intuition, because these greatly expanded boundaries of thought go far beyond direct experience and maybe the intellect as well.

In human dimensions, the Gaian perspective implies relationships that emphasize interdependence, seeing ourselves part of, but not controlling, the whole. The key is to transcend past polarizations and separations and to recognize the importance of all parts as they interrelate into an ever-more complex synthesis. In doing this, we would be moving toward community in the truest sense. This connectedness becomes the first law of ecology. It leads to redefining priorities. At the heart of our current culture, however, is the assumption that progress means unlimited growth—increasing production, consumption, income. There have been great leaps in enhancing the material standard of living in both capitalist and socialist countries. In mainstream terms, we see this as pursuing the "good life." But now this growth is jeopardizing our very existence.

Early in the 1970s, those on the alternative track began making long-range projections. They saw the flaws in the maximum growth model, satisfying our wants but not our real needs. They saw that education is concerned mainly with conformity, indoctrination, discipline—only the growth of the intellect rather than of the whole person—which carries over into how we see the workplace and business ethics. What happened to stimulating individual creativity, expression, and imagination? Then some people began to turn around the norms of competition and the adversarial win-lose mode. If we truly believe we're all connected, they said, we must find ways for all to benefit.

In terms of spiritual orientation, some of these communities hark back to pre-Roman Celtic Christianity, where God is felt to be present in nature. This doesn't necessarily mean worshiping nature, however. It's the holistic view where the collective mind is seen as very powerful, where there's the idea that everything "thinks." This is very different from Roman Christianity, which teaches an external, distant, all-powerful God and where proponents look for perfection outside the self. The Roman church vigorously proceeded to stamp out the Celtic enclaves since they couldn't control them with their centralized authority.

Today we're hearing more about the perennial wisdom, a distillation of the experiences of many philosophic explorers over thousands of years. It contains concepts and principles found in all major religions, based on universal spiritual experience. It includes identifying with one's core self and following that lead.

Peter Caddy, a cofounder of Findhorn, taught us to "learn to love where you are, what you're doing, and who you're with." He leaned heavily on the Laws of Manifestation that David Spangler articulated: "When we align our own will in harmony with that of the greater good, we open a doorway of wholeness to have our own needs met. Have faith, give thanks. As we receive, we give back. In this way we become part of a flow of love and abundance within creation." It's knowing that one possesses nothing but has a stewardship relationship with everything.

Those of us who went to Findhorn in the 1970s got a clear sense that our culture stands at a critical point between the death of most patterns familiar to us and the difficult birth of some entirely new configurations. The old ways were going fast, from family patterns to habits of energy consumption forced on us by the exponential degradation of our environment. We saw that the issue isn't stopping growth but seeing a new kind of growth: sustainable development that is fulfilling our material and social needs of today without compromising the needs of future generations. It has to do with how we use energy, grow our food, choose what we eat, build our homes, and decide what kind of cars to drive and what appliances to use. Our lifestyle patterns will have to change, with behavior that recognizes the new responsibility that goes along with living in an interdependent global community.

LIFESTYLE CHANGES CALLED FOR

There has been a trend toward moving to small towns and rural areas, away from cities and suburbs—although more recently we're also seeing a return to the city and the creation of pedestrian villages where residents can walk or bike to facilities.

People are questioning not only the high-tech urban rat race, but they also see the goal of ever-rising material wealth in our mass consumption, industrial society as simply no longer very realistic, despite what advertisers tell us.

What are some other lifestyle changes for the new era? We're already seeing more preventive and holistic health care as the role of the mind is being recognized—treating the whole person and taking more responsibility for our own bodies. The fitness movement is getting high visibility. There's a call for more organically and locally grown foods. We're talking about "regenerative agriculture," replenishing the soil and using natural pest controls and nutrients.

Back in the 1950s, we who were coming of age then were tempted by the daring ideas of anarchism and existentialism because we were so fed up with the status quo, so alienated from our homogeneous, flat culture. Two decades later some of us grabbed onto the sensational story of the Findhorn garden, with its frisson of communing with unseen forces in nature and the ability to sense a living kernel of consciousness in all life. This is what pulled a growing cadre in Wisconsin to want to experience those same awakenings here. We felt a budding sensitivity to environmental degradation, linking this to an almost animistic view of plants and the need to protect and listen to them.

We had an "anything goes" tolerance, embracing (at least the trappings of) all manner of spiritual practices, especially Far Eastern and American Indian. We looked across the ocean at the exotic locale of Findhorn, which was reigniting the leftover countercultural fervor of the '60s when young people kicked over the traces of convention and decorum and rules, indiscriminately throwing out whatever belief systems were mainstream. This meant people were ready for the open-ended spirituality of Findhorn, where all paths to enlightenment felt comfortable, whether they were known credos or no belief at all; where everyone could come together in silent group meditation that bypassed particular systems and dogmas; where one could simply open to spirit or inner awareness and acknowledge and trust the guidance that came as intuitive wisdom.

I should emphasize again that this hunger we found throughout our area for some kind of spiritual meaning is not universal within the community orbit. I was warned that to many, and not only in the mainstream, I, or we, would seem to be "from Mars." But in our experience, this search was real and widespread, and it was strong.

AWARENESS OF ALTERNATIVES HELPS TO BIRTH HIGH WIND

It was this pervasive belief in the interconnectedness of all life, so strong at Findhorn, that provided the inspiration, the reason for High Wind. It has been the experience with our land—these meadows and hills and woods—that fosters a personal sense of peace, of deepening, and often of healing and clarity in ordering priorities. Wendell Berry has noted that we're the only species that doesn't understand the need for cooperation and balance with nature. Some people are beginning to work at this deficiency.

What started as a dream that would set a course for my own life awakened a longing in many others, and each one brought his or her own idea of what such a "utopia" might look like. Actually, it was less a picture of utopia than a spark ignited in the hearts of a long procession of people who over the years have been drawn to High Wind. It was a light that showed each of us how we might contribute to creating a safer, saner, more humane world. Each brought a piece of this dream, and soon it became a collective vision, impossible for any one person to actualize alone but perhaps possible when gifts and talents were pooled.

It started with the search for the "good life" discussed above (the *real* one, not that of more money, a big house, and an accumulation of shiny "stuff"). It means a better way to live for a society going awry. What helped High Wind take off was that the time was exactly right in our area. In the mid-1970s and early 1980s, a lot more people were starting to question and doubt long-held, conventional beliefs that had always been taken for granted.

Finally, let me say that in pulling together notes from countless talks I've given, background materials I've compiled for High Wind, lectures and meetings I've attended, and publications I've read, I find it nearly impossible to remember exactly where some of the phrasing in this piece came from. Here are the names of just a few of the fellow explorers, thinkers, and authors who have spurred us on, a number of whom Bel and I have known well: David Spangler, Milenko Matanovic, William Irwin Thompson, Marilyn Ferguson, Fritz Schumacher, Corinne McLaughlin, Gordon Davidson, David Bohm, Rupert Sheldrake, Willis Harman, Paul Hawken, Peter and Eileen Caddy and other key Findhorn contacts, Dorothy Maclean, John and Nancy Todd, Barbara Marx Hubbard, Hazel Henderson, Robert Theobald, Ken Wilber, Jim Merkel, Joe Domingus and the "Ultimate Vehicle" gang, Wendell Berry, Wes Jackson, Miriam McGillis, Thomas Berry, Bill McKibben, Aldo Leopold, Laird Schaub and other members in the Fellowship for Intentional Community, Amory Lovins, David Orr, Peter Russell, Fritjof Capra, Lester Brown, Joseph Campbell, Scott and Helen Nearing, Guy and Laura Waterman, Carl McDaniel—and probably fifty more I can't think of at the moment. These were some of the pioneers whose ideas began by floating disembodied in the ethers, the products of minds that refused to fall into line, pioneers who are now bringing together more and more converts who see that we must break free to form the critical mass for real change.

> Our world needs a lot of High Winds.... High Wind was a lot of good, committed people wanting to do the right thing.
>
> — *Pamm Steffen, High Wind program participant, 2005 High Wind Survey*

Reflections on Bridging the Gap between "What Is" and "What Might Be"—Between Mainstream and Prophetic Thinking from Observers and Participants in the Intentional Community Movement

In 2005, the High Wind Board of Directors sent a survey to 180 people who had lived in the community or had participated in High Wind activities. Some of the comments below are taken from responses to that survey.

Question: What would it take to translate holistic and planetary ideas into public policy—ideas that clearly reflect sustainability, cooperation, empowerment, interdependence? What would be needed to give the federal government a comprehensive operational set of policy recommendations that would challenge the obsolete framework now used?

Answer: It would take some clear thinkers looking at the world in new ways, some hardheaded holistic-minded government insiders working on the front line, a well-thought-out communications/marketing strategy for bringing new models into the public domain, some money, and a nucleus of committed, energetic people crazy enough to believe that the time is ripe to bring a new value context into government and who are courageous enough risk-takers to help make it happen."
> — *Belden Paulson, introducing his report on the meeting of sixty national and world leaders at the United Nations in October 1987, to explore the concept of a New Synthesis Think Tank, Windwatch, January 1988*

We see in our country a great deal of specialization, of single-issue orientation. People are doing excellent jobs focusing on the important areas of ecology, health, peace, public policy, self-development. Perhaps communities, because they are small, relatively manageable entities, are uniquely suited for trying to integrate the various strands. When people see how all the parts are connected, we can transcend the turf conflicts and form coalitions where we cooperate rather than compete. Then we're on our way to a sustainable country and a sustainable world."
> — *Lisa Paulson, from the editorial "Why Does High Wind Exist?" Windwatch, Fall/Winter 1988*

What's really important is radical stuff, and most politicians assume there is no constituency for such matters. . . . We need to break out of the conceptual prisons that have made us rigid and conformist so we can reshape the intellectual and political landscape.
> — *Comments from the October 1987 think tank gathering in New York, as reported by Belden Paulson, Windwatch, January 1988*

On the one hand, there is obviously a trend of "shutting down" of ecological/liberal/open-minded/international thinking [in this country]. We see a remarkable growth of individuality and resistance

to communal living. On the other hand, people in various spiritual communities are trying to create a larger network, almost underground, to help change this situation in the culture (if we still can). Between disillusionment with intentional communities and the persistent growth of "dogmatic" or more traditionally-oriented communes (ashrams, Buddhist centers), it's probably hard to make people aware of something new/fresh/more in tune with the general/broader spiritual evolution.
  — *Metka Zupancic, 2005 High Wind Survey*

Some of us will go to any length to avoid using the cliché "New Age" because it has become jargon, is branded elitist, is misused and overused. Yet whatever it is, it's an identifiable "underground swell" whose adherents recognize each other immediately, even when conventional communication is hampered by language barriers. There's something else going on at another level. It's a sleeping giant of knowing that lives somewhere in a great many consciousnesses. In some it is acknowledged and bursts out, in others it is dormant or anesthetized by the predominant cultures across the globe. Because it's still a minority paradigm, it is "elite"—careful, discriminating, prophetic, yes, but not exclusive. When others are ready, they see it too. What we're about is sprouting many tiny specks of this awareness on the globe that will gradually fill in the spaces until we're no longer the elite few, but old hat mainstream.
  — *Lisa Paulson, after a six-week trip across Europe visiting alternative centers, noting the instant recognition among the people encountered, Windwatch, February 1985.*

Human nature and behavior are what they are and change at an annoyingly slow pace. . . . However, I think, overall, human consciousness is indeed changing, whether through actual learning or through growth of the spirit and soul. But like the ant who moved a rubber tree plant, we have to maintain our high hopes and just keep plugging away in whatever fashion we can to raise consciousness. It will make a difference.
  — *Alan Zuberbuehler, 2005 High Wind Survey*

In essence, High Wind to me is "a happening." More than a nonprofit organization, or a farm in the Kettle Moraine, or a bioshelter and domes, or a group of Associates around the world, or a small, live-in community on forty-six acres, or an unending series of educational events and small-scale research projects, it is a moment of history. We're waking up. As we leaf through the great stages in the history of civilization, there are long periods of stability or gradual change. These are punctuated by short periods of critical change. . . . Millions today are awakening not only to the current great world crises, but also to the great opportunities. . . . Maybe the real action, human genius, the R & D that takes place when a few committed people with boundless energy and imagination unite, is found in small groups that "happen" to come together. They "happen" to set in motion some sort of process that penetrates the mysteries of existence in seemingly unexplained ways.
  — *Belden Paulson, Windwatch, January 1984*

Chapter Four

The Birth and Unfolding of High Wind

People need to feel connected in a real way to their innermost knowing, and High Wind can provide that entry point and ground it in "good work." In this way High Wind could begin to envision itself less as a place, than as an idea whose time has come for a larger integration to take place.

— *George Schricker, High Wind visitor and supporter,* Windwatch, *April 1987*

I've related how my own journey to community kicked into high gear with my 1976 visit to Findhorn. My first hurdle on returning was to convince my skeptical, feet-on-the-ground, professor husband that something profound and valid was indeed happening in Scotland. After meeting some of the key players—Findhorn founder Peter Caddy and members of Lorian—Bel was not only impressed but fully engaged.

A HUNGER FOR CHANGE: GATHERING THE TROOPS

Early in 1977, Bel and I were tapped to be part of a Chicago group organizing a national ecological conference for March that was to be keynoted by *Small is Beautiful* author Fritz Schumacher. I gave a presentation about Findhorn that surprised everyone by drawing one of the larger crowds. One of Bel's university deans was present and immediately saw the relevance of the issues I raised. He urged Bel to set up courses around these themes. In fact, through the ensuing years, Bel's position and influence in the university system was crucial to not only getting legitimate

sponsorship of most of our programs, but also in helping to bridge the enormous gap between a very mainstream institution and concepts that at the time were definitely on the outer fringes.

As I mentioned in Chapter Two, in June 1977, the University of Wisconsin-Milwaukee brought Peter and Eileen Caddy, Findhorn's founders, to speak. Their appearance flushed twelve hundred people out of the woodwork and ignited a fire under a huge cadre of enthusiasts (as well as the curious) from all over our part of the Midwest.

The clout that Bel was able to wield didn't manifest overnight: in the 1960s, he had watched the racial crisis exploding and escalating across the river in Milwaukee's inner city and persuaded his bosses at both UW-Milwaukee and University Extension in Madison of the urgency to respond. They created a new department focused on urban poverty and racism, which he chaired for twenty-two years. In the latter 1970s, he combined this subject matter with futures studies; his programming expanded "alternative education" with peace studies, sustainable futures, and new thinking about politics and learning.

In 1978, the Lorian group that had come together at Findhorn with David Spangler and Milenko Matanovic moved to Milwaukee to teach with us. We tackled variations on rather esoteric subjects—such as how spirit works in our culture and the "Who am I?" and "What is my life about?" questions. It wasn't easy to convince the academic dons to place two people on the faculty who didn't hold doctorates, but Bel noted that they were world-recognized figures and that no one else on the faculty could teach what they knew.

Bel managed to incorporate new course titles into university offerings. Our first class, for credit and noncredit, attracted a record 120 participants; it was titled "Planetary Survival and the Role of Alternative Communities." Over the next six years, David and Milenko taught academic classes with us. They held our hands as we launched the High Wind Association, which I'll describe shortly.

Thanks to his introduction to the revolutionary thinking of the visiting Caddys and our new Lorian teaching cadre, it had become clear to Bel that massive societal change was called for, and he was moving quickly to raise awareness in our local area. Yet, until now, he himself had not been directly exposed to the catalyst for all this ferment—the vortex of ideas and example that had so effectively changed my direction. He had not been to Findhorn.

As the activity in Milwaukee heated up, we both began to realize that this was the next essential step. In spring 1978, Bel signed up for Findhorn's "Experience Week," the intensive program in which a group of about fifteen visitors at a time

were introduced to every facet of the community (a program I had gone through earlier). Mornings and evenings, participants met with key leaders to hear about Findhorn's history and philosophy, its organization, economics, governance, and spiritual life. Afternoons, they pitched in to work in the gardens and kitchens and construction projects, getting an even closer sense of how this extensive experiment played out by conversing and laboring shoulder to shoulder with community residents. There were field trips to places of great beauty and spiritual significance.

I had arrived at Findhorn a week earlier than Bel, enrolling in a workshop, "Creating a Center of Light." Peter Caddy was a principal teacher, detailing the steps for building a successful spiritually based enclave. Then, while Bel was involved with his "Experience" program, I spent the week as a "working guest." Along the way, we were both delighted to get the inside scoop from Angelynn Brown. As I mentioned at the end of Chapter Two, Angelynn was a former community member whose inner guidance had propelled her to Milwaukee soon after my first trip in 1976. Her mission was to form spiritual study groups and help interpret the message of Findhorn with me. Angelynn was now living at our house and had gone back to Scotland for a brief visit.

A two-month trip to Findhorn in spring 1979, sponsored by UW-Milwaukee, was critical to solidifying understanding and more widespread support for our goals. An enthusiastic group signed on; some had participated in almost all of our growing number of local educational offerings, while others from across the U.S. and Canada responded to advertisements. Our son Eric, recently graduated from college, was part of the group. I led this band of twenty-three, ranging in age from nineteen to early seventies. We coalesced in London and then proceeded to Scotland. The Findhorn leadership rallied to design a stunning program for us, exposing our people to an inside look at every aspect of community life and its radical ideology. We were told it was the first cooperative venture with a major university, a significant benchmark. After a month in the main community in northeast Scotland, some of our group opted to bus across the country to spend time on the primitive Isle of Erraid, off the west coast in the Inner Hebrides. Erraid is a tiny island under Findhorn's custodianship, with fewer than a dozen inhabitants scratching out their subsistence from the bleak, rocky landscape. Bel flew to Findhorn for wrap-up sessions where it became clear that the entire experience had been not only highly inspiring but life changing for most of our folks. In fact, it was many members of this trip who went on to become the backbone of High Wind's mission as it unfolded and flowered.

Out of the early classes, a dedicated core of supporters formed—about fifty people of all ages—who came to the courses, weekend workshops, and national conferences we offered from 1977 to 1980.

> Initially, when I first stuck my toe in the High Wind waters, I knew I was open to self-growth; I just didn't really have much of an idea where this would lead me. My relationship with High Wind and the people of High Wind is highly valued and helps create a balance for me. I have clearly been stretched in "possibilities" by High Wind.
>
> — *Tom McGinnity, High Wind program leader, 2005 High Wind Survey*

After a while, they began to tell us it wasn't enough to just *talk* about the world crises—there was an urgent need to *do* something that would be a concrete demonstration of new ways of living. Time was running out. Specifically, the students wanted to show how we could live more benignly on the earth by constructing energy-efficient buildings that didn't consume fossil fuels.

On weekends, Bel and I began to bring fifteen to twenty of these core participants up to the countryside near Plymouth, where we owned a rundown old farmhouse without running water. Located on forty-six acres at the edge of the Northern Kettle Moraine State Forest, it was fifty miles from the bustle of the city. With glorious, long views twenty miles out over rolling, glacial moraine pastureland dotted with silos, this was a place where we could dream together while starting to renovate the crumbling farm buildings.

It was an ambience where in winter majestic walls of snow and sheets of dazzling ice crystals would give way in spring and summer to a soft green forest and prairie grasses blowing freely across the wide meadows. There were lands ready to absorb the eager spirit of love and cooperation of their new caretakers and then, as we would discover, give back a palpable healing energy.

We gutted a chicken coop and turned it into an insulated post-and-beam solar hostel where people could stay (the "Coop de Ville"). We built a primitive plastic greenhouse on the south side of the farmhouse to store heat and grow tomatoes and greens. The pounding of nails and hauling of soil and rocks was always accompanied by animated conversation and strategizing. It became clear that if we were talking about people cooperating with nature, this conviction should affect how we grow our food and build our houses.

The group was especially interested in solar power as a result of the energy crisis of 1973, and together we drew up a proposal and applied to the U.S. Department of Energy for a grant to construct a demonstration building— a passive solar bioshelter like the "arks" we'd visited at New Alchemy, pioneered in the 1970s. This could be a significant experiment, because our Wisconsin climate is even harsher than that along the Atlantic Ocean. To our surprise, in late 1980, we were awarded a small, $25,000 Appropriate Technology Grant, one of the last before the Reagan administration shut down this program.

> I believe High Wind can provide a pivot point, an entry, for those who are feeling disenfranchised and are waiting in the wings for the opportunity to enter into useful communion with the world of "good work," as E.F. Schumacher puts it.
> — *George Schricker, visitor and supporter,*
> *Windwatch, April 1987*

SEED MONEY AND A LEGAL IDENTITY— MANDATE TO MOVE

The award, although modest, was the catalyst needed to galvanize us into action. Enough dreaming. With grant money in hand, we wrote our first invitational brochure, laying out the broad strokes of our vision. We included some of the concepts I'd seen at both Findhorn and New Alchemy, bringing together the spiritual and the ecological.

Bel and I set up a meeting in early 1981 at Kenwood Methodist church in Milwaukee, and over one hundred people showed up. Almost immediately, several folks stepped forward, volunteering to help. In the beginning, we didn't think of ourselves as creating a "community" (too pretentious). Rather, we were simply a task group committing to construct a demonstration building and, tangentially, to tend a large organic vegetable garden to feed the crew. A carpenter said he'd been looking for an opportunity like this and could move out to the farm immediately to organize the building of the bioshelter. A newspaper librarian with an ancillary passion for new technologies proposed coming to live in the chicken coop, cutting his hours in half and joining the work crew. A teacher offered to move out at the end of the school year to grow a garden to feed the group. In the first few months, some half-dozen people arrived to live at what we had started to call High Wind Farm.

We'd known earlier we were going to do *something*, even if it was still all pretty vague. To be ready for this stage, in 1977 we'd created a nonprofit organization called the High Wind Association. The name held meanings on several levels: we were certainly generating high energy around some lofty ideals and goals. Also, we found wind to be a significant companion, whistling frequently across our exposed high plateau.

And so High Wind was born. First, there had been my great enthusiasm, my passion for this idea, which I had spoken about widely after the Findhorn experience. Then came Bel's crucial vision and influence that could channel far-out new theories and paradigms through the staid academic system to build a working base. The glamorous presence and wisdom provided by the Lorian contingent served as a powerful magnet for interested people. Bel and I were the initial catalysts, but ultimately it was the faithful band of compatriots who persevered, who supported and pushed us to create a solid experiment, who brought their ideals and hammers that made it happen.

Bel and I kicked off the project by donating an acre of land just east of the farmhouse for the new building, and we made available the entire farm for experimental work.

The concept of the bioshelter was that of a micro-farm: a greenhouse and residence combined under one roof, embodying intimate cooperation between people and nature. With interconnecting, closed-loop growing systems and heat storage, it would be designed to *produce* rather than consume energy. It would show that the energy and power of the sun was free and unlimited, a gift from the universe to everyone.

The excitement of these first recruits who put aside their other lives and come to build was catching. Soon many more came to High Wind to join in—families and singles—for a few days or a few weeks or longer. Volunteers showed up each weekend to supplement the small residential group, and the bioshelter began to go up. For several years, we continued to refine our goals and strategize while we labored, raising walls, cutting and fitting drywall, laying shingles on the roof.

"EDUCATION" REDEFINED

Thus began our wonderful, often rough, mostly exhilarating ride into the world of communal living. We built the bioshelter, farmed, and started cottage industries (furniture-making, desktop publishing, a shop selling crafts and books). The cornerstone of all our work, though, was *education*: exploring and sharing ideas about living with grace and integrity, and cooperating conscientiously with nature. (Unlike the traditional Christian idea that humans have dominion over nature, we felt strongly that we were an integral part of a large, connected whole.) To this end, we continued to offer the classes that we had begun in Milwaukee, and at the same time, we ramped up offerings at the farm.

Weekend workshops and seminars (still mostly cosponsored with the university) covered a range of topics, from the pragmatic to the philosophical: ecological architecture, ethnobotany, ayurvedic cooking, Native American culture and crafts, new politics, permaculture techniques to integrate human lifestyles with natural systems, ruminations and projections on the nature of spirit .... Bel liked to characterize High Wind as a three-legged stool: addressing matters of spirit, education, and technology.

It was clear that our inspiration for High Wind thus came out of both the ecological thrust of New Alchemy and the spiritual grounding of Findhorn, in cooperation with the University of Wisconsin and other educational institutions. People of every age came to envisage alternative futures and new models of community. The learning usually happened in unorthodox, informal ways, not only during scheduled lectures and discussions but while hauling rocks or nailing up boards or chopping vegetables. Some came for formal programs, others to work as volunteers as a respite from the pressures of the city. We always emphasized the practical advantages of group living—how there was sharing on a broad scale, from food to fuel. How we could keep more money in the community by selling products and skills to each other. Barter, we told them, was common (such as a sewing job for figuring taxes). We could help each other build our living spaces and homes, and we weren't stuck with high rents or mortgages. One could live very well at High Wind on a few thousand dollars a year. The bonus was that all this could take place among a group of caring, like-minded friends.

For a number of years, from the early to the latter 1980s, we ran a semester-long course for university credit, known as the Living/Learning Seminar in Three Communities. Students spent a month at High Wind, a month at Findhorn in Scotland, and a month at either Sirius in Massachusetts or Eourres in the French Alps. Approximately a dozen students of all ages participated in each of these three-month seminars,

creating their own small community against the backdrops of the three larger intentional communities. (Note that when speaking about these seminars, we often shortened the name to the Three-Community Seminar.)

We held the first of our summer "Lorian Seminars" in 1981, led by David Spangler, who had set Findhorn on its path before coming to this country. High Wind continued to offer these seminars for twelve years with the same dynamic group of teachers/writers/world-class thinkers. In fact, participants in this first Lorian gathering were on hand at the significant moment of initiating the bioshelter construction. I'm sure the burly operators of cement mixers hovering over the excavated hole were astonished and bemused to see some forty people (including many young women in shorts and halters) scurrying around shoveling wet cement into wooden forms for the foundation!

WHO AND WHAT WERE WE?

By the end of the first year, there were a dozen residents (twenty-two at our peak), and we realized we needed to pause in the midst of almost frenzied physical, "macho" activities to deal with the growing challenges of getting along and making group decisions—the blood and guts of what communities are about. We woke up (finally!) to the realization that we were indeed a community, an *intentional* community, a group of people with shared values who had come together to live and work for a common purpose.

High Wind found it had to make a major decision about agreeing on just what this common purpose was. Would we be a homesteading community (separating from the mainstream to pursue a more "pure" lifestyle), or would we be open to the public and follow a path of education and service? With more and more visitors descending and more educational offerings, there was an increasing strain on the facilities—especially on the residents who had to deal with the complicated logistics of being around mobs of people.

As an aside, Bel and I were still coming out to High Wind only on weekends. We weren't able to move to the country full time until we built our own solar house in 1986. We spent longer chunks of time there during the summer, though, when we had many programs. We were always deeply involved in almost every aspect of the community, whether or not we were actually sleeping there.

There were elements of homesteading in how all of us functioned and thought about ourselves (hunkering down to be as self-sufficient as possible), but we decided in the end we *did* want to continue sharing whatever we were discovering— what worked and what didn't: the educational aspect through demonstrations, workshops, seminars, tours of High Wind, writing and dialoguing about what we were learning. (A couple of years later some of the group opted for more privacy and splintered off to create their own community.)

Besides reflecting our values and purpose, and fulfilling the rationale for our nonprofit status, the educational programs were High Wind's bread and butter. What small surplus was left after covering the cost of an event was our only real income and went toward maintaining the basic infrastructure of the community. Most people served as volunteers.

Who were these first "settlers" at High Wind, most of whom had answered the call at our first meeting in Milwaukee? There was Jim Priest, our lead carpenter, who'd been on a karma yoga path and had dreamed of joining an ecological village and simplifying his lifestyle. Betsy Abert had wanted to live in closer attunement with nature; she was reticent about acknowledging the spiritual in herself yet functioned instinctively with caring straight from the heart. She canceled a teaching contract and came to plant French intensive vegetable beds. Alida Sherman was a PhD psychologist attracted to the idea of networking—linking a political/philosophical worldview to hands-on demonstrations; she organized our kitchen and made order out of the mélange of folks who bunked in the farmhouse.

John and Cindy Smithson and their two young daughters wanted to combine wilderness training with a spiritual approach for youth; the first family to come, their skills were handcrafts, raising animals, and coping with logistics. David Lagerman, a research librarian with the *Milwaukee Journal*, revealed a true renaissance temperament; he especially loved to tinker with alternative technologies, became deadly serious about conservation, found he was a born teacher, and was always trying to correlate our actions as individuals and groups with how our level of consciousness was evolving.

Todd Broadie and Cindy Moran came with an almost clinical curiosity about dissecting the dynamics of communal life (along with researching dolphin intelligence). They had been grad students at UW-Madison. Chet and Sue Tippett exemplified hardy, simple living and offered much practical know-how in mechanics and organic growing. Priscilla Dean was coming off a marriage and her job as a school principal; she contributed an energy of love and fun, and turned out to be a diligent carpenter.

There was my husband, Bel, who had established a refugee village in Italy, worked with the United Nations in Rome, conducted social/economic/political research in Northeast Brazil, moved to Wisconsin as a professor of political science, then created a university department to address Milwaukee's central city problems. Eventually he moved on to the field of futures studies and began contemplating what it would take to bring about fundamental societal change or "transformation" (the sweeping buzzword of the early '80s). Bel has always had a special gift for seeing possibilities for a project when no one else does, and he can lay out the precise, even risky, steps to initiate that project. His contagious confidence rubs off on those around him, who get excited, and as a group they become the critical mass to carry the job forward.

Finally, there was me. I loved playing with words through writing and speaking. Always anxious to help others see and become excited by the possibilities I was seeing, I found I could galvanize enthusiasm and spark imaginations, and even rattle a few souls. As High Wind took shape, Bel and I made a pretty good team. Where I tended

to leap passionately into situations, he remained unruffled, undaunted, clear-headed. I might come up with an idea and frame it in evocative language, and then he could turn that vision into a coherent way to move forward—a significant mission, or even an irresistible grail. I'd be there, running with whatever was happening and recording the proceedings—another lifelong compulsion of mine. I was also deeply drawn to creating connections with spirit in nature, amplified by my exposure to the practices at Findhorn—and, of course, it was the power of community I found at Findhorn that began the chain of events that had almost inevitably led to an experiment like High Wind.

As we were deciding who we were, what we stood for, and what we aspired to, we penned the High Wind credo. It's a simple statement by the first intrepid pioneers that "covers the bases" and to which, to this day, we keep coming back when we need to clarify and remind ourselves of our ongoing mission:

> *To walk lightly on the earth,*
> *To know the spirit within,*
> *To hear our fellow beings,*
> *To invoke the light of wisdom, and*
>
> *To build the future now.*

STRATEGIES FOR GETTING ALONG AND FOR GETTING BY

As with all other communities we know, we started a life of many meetings. Our decisions were made by consensus, so meetings were often very long, some even lasting a couple of days, as we talked and talked until everyone could agree. We saw the need for such discussions because tensions could run high when, for example, kids left wet towels on the communal bathroom floor (raising the sticky issue of group parenting). There needed to be some agreement about diet as some members were junk food addicts while others were fussy vegetarians. Also Jim, our bioshelter "focalizer," wanted everybody up and out carrying concrete blocks or nailing Sheetrock at 6 a.m., when a few, like one cerebral couple, preferred to read and practice yoga half the night and then sleep in.

So there were plenty of interpersonal conflicts and divergent styles and habits to be negotiated. After a while, we instituted business meeting times to decide nitty-gritty issues and separate "community building" meetings (à la Scott Peck) to work through emotional upsets and personality "stuff." This worked fairly well because we could tackle issues in the business meetings with dispatch (satisfying the "get-it-done" types), and spend more time letting out feelings in the community building meetings (satisfying the "process" types who encouraged everybody to vent freely).

Early on, we created a board of directors, drawing from among both the residents and outside supporters. This didn't happen easily, as there was considerable protest from some residents who thought the central focus of the work was in the country; they couldn't trust outsiders to have a say in the affairs out there. The rhetoric of "equal decision-making" was different from the reality the residents perceived. Those living full time at High Wind saw themselves as the core of the organization, while Bel and I also had a base in Milwaukee and were tied to enthusiasts in a broad circle—the "larger High Wind"—whose financial and moral support was essential.

A few recognized there were legal and financial matters and other major Association decisions that a board needed to be responsible for that went beyond the group of current residents, some of whom were fairly transient. Members tended to stay for two to five years, some for only a few months (viewing High Wind a bit like a "school" where they would learn and then move on). Others found this to be a way of life that made sense and where they wanted to build homes and put down roots, committing to be here perhaps for the rest of their lives. The upshot of the discussion about forming a board was that the farm residents would decide issues of daily life but the "planetary agenda" and major financial outlays, educational planning, and personnel matters would come under the new board, which, of course, also did include some residents.

> I came to High Wind impressively ill-equipped to be a leader. I certainly didn't have the skills. I came out of a school where the most important thing was not to insult or hurt anyone's feelings, not to inconvenience anyone—to be silent and put on a good face, to smile even when I was dying inside or felt anger, to be brave and long-suffering. Needless to say, this didn't prepare me for life in an intentional community, where honest communication and saying the hard things are usually the only way it can work.
>
> — Lisa Paulson, in "A Note to My Community," February 1991

Eventually, this division of responsibilities was accepted by everyone; we all recognized that there were pressing everyday matters to be shepherded by those on-site who didn't have the time or inclination to take on the longer-range planning and shaping of educational events. They were also often too close to operations on the ground (and to their own empty pockets) to envision large monetary commitments.

There was always the thorny question of how the residents could support themselves. Beyond the government grant that paid only for the initial bioshelter building materials, we were dependent on volunteer labor. High Wind had minimal funds to pay anyone anything, except for small amounts to cover speakers, food, and the people who did the work during large events. Taxes, insurance, and repairs were covered by Bel and me.

A footnote: at first we'd thought that because we were incorporated as a legal 501(C) (3) non-profit organization with an educational purpose, we wouldn't have to pay property taxes on the bioshelter and its one acre. However, our petition was denied because we weren't going to hold regular daily classes. This issue had created such a heated reaction in our little township of Mitchell that, in the interest of smooth local relations, we quickly decided not to contest the ruling and agreed to pay. (A dozen years later, though, I found the rumor still circulating that we'd never paid taxes.)

Those living at High Wind found various ways to stay afloat. Some had saved a small nest egg. Others found part-time jobs in the area. There were couples where one partner worked outside the community while the other was a full-time volunteer. (For example, because Bel taught at the university, I could devote all my time to being the outreach person and could garden, run tours, and edit our journal, *Windwatch*, which chronicled what we were doing and thinking.) Then there were some residents who thought if we were here to demonstrate simple living, it made little sense to commute away from the land, and they looked for ways to earn a livelihood on site. Don Austin, a retired school principal from Chicago, had always wanted to work with his hands, so he created a shop in one of our barns and built futons, eventually opening a store in Milwaukee to sell his woodcraft.

A young couple, Peter and Bernadette Seely, arrived with their small baby, with the hope of pursuing organic agriculture. Eventually they started what we believe was one of the first CSA (Community Supported Agriculture) programs in the Midwest, selling produce directly to individuals on a subscription-delivery basis. The subscribers (now more than eight hundred) become involved in supporting the farmers who grow their food; often they come out to help plant and harvest. Jan Masaros (now Christensen) came to High Wind in the late 1980s with sophisticated computer knowledge and set up a desktop publishing business with David Lagerman's wife, Louise Mann. Marcia Kjos created a weaving studio and shop to sell crafts and books in the basement of the bioshelter. A few of our folks worked part time at High Wind Books, a store established in Milwaukee in 1984, both to showcase our work and to make alternative ideas, books, and materials available in the city.

Besides those mentioned above, the long roster of full-time volunteer residents—couples, singles, kids—added immensely to the richness of the community over the years. You'd find them digging in the gardens, splitting wood, tending farm animals, struggling with paperwork, anchoring our spiritual and celebratory life, becoming pivotal "go-to" resources, mediating disputes, carpentering/renovating the buildings, holding the kitchen together, meeting visitors and running tours, and always sprucing up and beautifying forgotten corners.

Bel and I contributed to a description of High Wind in Corinne McLaughlin and Gordon Davidson's book, *Builders of the Dawn* (Stillpoint Publishing, 1985):

> Essentially, High Wind stands for an ecological ethic that embraces cooperation and stewardship on all levels, connecting people, buildings, land, spirit. Our gardeners are sensitive to the interdependence (and beauty) of plants, soil, insects, and wildlife. The forms and energies in the natural surroundings become creative partners and inspiration for our artists. High Wind builders learn that esthetics and technical efficiency are equally important. Visitors or students, who may come initially to see the bioshelter, find this effort to balance physical projects with the energies of people and of the land into a harmonious whole, is what makes High Wind a truly valid experiment.

(High-flown, perhaps, but at least this was what we stood for and strove for!)

GAINING SKILLS, IN TASKS AND ATTITUDES

At first, everybody in the community did everything together. We got to wear many hats and learned multiple skills—as builders, gardeners, cooks, group and event facilitators, communicators. Gradually, though, members began to specialize and, as the years piled up, besides the educational programs that involved us all, the various private businesses mentioned above were created, both at High Wind and in Milwaukee.

Roles in the community were not sexist; there were very competent women farmers and men who enjoyed cooking. There was no pressure for guys to be "manly." In fact, we women were happy to see the men become more vulnerable, showing feelings, being demonstrative. In our first year, however, an incident of the men asserting raw power over women shook everyone and taught us to be extra vigilant lest this happen again.

The episode involved certain design elements of the bioshelter mandated by Lillian Leenhouts, our volunteer architect, a nationally known solar expert. One of these was the use of concrete decking for the greenhouse loft space to provide thermal mass, as well as being more durable and moisture resistant than wood. Jim and David, in charge of construction, chose to completely ignore this directive. They brushed aside Betsy and me, protesting angrily, and proceeded on their own to build the loft of wood. They said the donation of the Spancrete, which I'd negotiated, was just too late and they had already started nailing the trusses for the greenhouse floor. They claimed it wasn't a question of gender, but to us women, this certainly seemed to be a factor.

It came down to which one, Jim or Lillian—both furious—would pull out, and ultimately we knew we couldn't afford to lose Jim. At that point—and also over a critical change in the roof design without her knowledge—our architect stepped away from the project.

This incident really unnerved everyone and prompted us to look squarely at our interpersonal relationships. We committed to work seriously on destructive feelings and held special meetings just for "processing" them. We tried to be careful about criticizing each other, although reflecting both honestly and lovingly what we saw was part of the openness we sought, too. With the help of outside mediators who led us in eye-opening "active listening" exercises, and other often painful confrontations and admissions, we forced ourselves to take risks and found we couldn't hide our quirks, we couldn't play face-saving games or indulge in power plays. The result was that consciousness was definitely raised a few notches, and we stood a greater chance of shaping up in the personal growth department. We set out to transform negativity with caring and transparency and to understand better the synergy principle that the whole is greater than the sum of its parts. All this, of course, was the ideal and not easily accomplished, but it was the goal to which we were committed.

Glimpses of Findhorn and the Isle of Erraid

In 1978, I return to Findhorn, taking Bel for his first plunge into this rarified atmosphere. I plug in as a "working guest," and we reunite with Angelynn Brown, my indispensable colleague in spreading the new ideas in Milwaukee. A former community resident who had come to live with us, she's back at Findhorn. (Two years later my close friend becomes my daughter-in-law!)

A year later, in 1979, I return to Findhorn with a study group of twenty-three who have become very curious about this community. They are off with me to spend two months in the main community and at its offshoot, Erraid, a tiny island in the Inner Hebrides off Scotland's west coast.

Findhorn pulls out all the stops for our visit, one of its first large-scale educational programs launched in conjunction with an American university. Key community leaders share their vision and stories with us, and everyone gets an authentic feel for the life by laboring alongside residents in many of the twenty-six work departments. At Erraid, our Wisconsin group pitches in to dig and plant with a much smaller enclave that exists in survival mode, close to the harsh, rocky land they cultivate (mostly parsnips while we were there). Their lives are often determined by the whims of the roiling tides of the Sea of Iona surrounding their primitive isle.

Unusual stones characterize the Findhorn shore on the North Sea.

Lisa meets with Findhorn founders Peter and Eileen Caddy, 1978.

Bel's first time at Findhorn, he chats with Angelynn Brown, a former resident back for a visit, 1978. (She would later marry our son, Eric.)

Our 1979 study group works in the Findhorn herb garden with community residents, 1979.

Bel and our son, Eric, on sand dunes above the North Sea at Findhorn, 1979.

The 1979 study group arrives at the Isle of Erraid off the west coast of Scotland.

Hiking the cliffs and spotting seals on Erraid.

Digging and sorting potatoes on primitive Erraid.

Lisa spends the Erraid week working under the cold frame.

Seeds Are Planted: Momentum Builds for a Project in Wisconsin

Among an expanding group of enthusiasts, momentum builds around the Findhorn idea of connecting people, nature, and spirit, and also around the New Alchemy Institute's experimental work with renewable energy. It becomes clear that "something" is bursting to unfold in our region that combines these two thrusts. In the fall of 1977, we draw up a preliminary vision and purpose, and incorporate as a nonprofit organization we call the High Wind Association.

Since the group is pushing hard for a place to create a tangible demonstration of these principles, Bel and I offer the use of several dilapidated farm buildings on forty-six acres we own near Plymouth, Wisconsin, north of Milwaukee. The bucolic location, adjacent to the rolling Northern Kettle Moraine State Forest, evokes a deep sense of the oneness of all life, which the first volunteers and community members pick up on quickly. As we begin to actualize our dreams and schemes, we find ourselves tuning in to the needs of the land around us, flowing with the demands and offerings of each season.

Farmhouse and outbuildings, built in 1900, owned by the Paulsons before the first communitarians arrive, 1973.

High Wind Landscapes through the Seasons

The chittering and sleepy drone in the high oaks and hickories in summer, the dark earth beneath them giving up their loamy scents.

Golden light of autumn suffuses drifting leaves, and meadow milkweed pods break open to send off their silky white seed puffs.

Hiss of sleet driven across the exposed ridge and vast snow plain by screaming winter winds.

Then peepers singing in the valley pond below on spring evenings.

East vista from the high bioshelter ridge, 1983.

Eric creates boardwalks that traverse the soggy fen, 1995.

The bare bones of winter, 1972.

Trillium carpets the forest floor in May: two young communitarians, Niko and Lark Paulson, 1986.

I feel such a deep connection to the land, like my soul sunk a taproot into the earth where I first stepped foot on those windy hills for the living/learning seminar. I found my voice at High Wind. [It was] the one place and time I knew who I was.
— Elizabeth Matson,
    program participant,
    2005 High Wind Survey

Connection with others in a common goal. Connecting up nature and mother earth and becoming aware again of our oneness with her.
— Beth Herbert,
    program participant,
    2005 High Wind Survey

Evening on the prairie.

The Original High Wind Farmhouse

The earliest, very diverse, group of community residents crowd into the six bedrooms of the turn-of-the-century farmhouse (promptly dubbed the "pressure cooker"). Bel and I hustle to install indoor plumbing to replace the pump and outhouse in the yard, which had served the previous farm inhabitants for eighty years. Other High Wind folks carve out living quarters in the enormous barn that doubles as our classroom/meeting space, and in the scrubbed-out, retrofitted chicken coop. Our first solar experiment is a funky, Tedlar-glazed greenhouse on the sunny side of the farmhouse where vegetables can be grown in winter. Visitors and workshop participants, often from across the U.S., brave all weathers to reach this "community center." Soon we find ourselves feeding huge crowds out of the large country kitchen.

In February 1981, we call a meeting of our ardent fellow dreamers at Kenwood Methodist Church in Milwaukee (where five years before I was whirling and chanting as a Sufi initiate). On announcing receipt of the government grant to build a demonstration bioshelter, several folks step forward immediately to commit their help. Dropping out of mainstream jobs, they soon move to High Wind. Jim Priest signs on as lead carpenter and Alida Sherman organizes the kitchen. David Lagerman (who has already moved to the farm part time) becomes our technical coordinator. John Smithson brings his family of four, and Cindy Moran, with her partner Todd Broadie, follows shortly. The next summer Betsy Abert leaves her teaching job to plant a large garden to feed everyone.

All are volunteers; High Wind hasn't any extra money to pay anyone.

First solar application: a small Tedlar greenhouse to grow tomatoes and greens in winter, 1981.

The farmhouse as community center, 1987.

Building the Bioshelter

With advice from David Bergmark, architect for the New Alchemy Institute's pioneering "bioshelter" in Massachusetts, we submit a proposal for funds to construct our own bioshelter in Wisconsin. This will be a micro farm in a building combining residential space with a large, passive solar greenhouse—storing the sun's heat in five-hundred-gallon water tanks where fish can also be raised. In 1980 we're awarded a modest grant from the U.S. Department of Energy, sufficient to buy materials if the labor is supplied by volunteers.

We break ground in 1981 during the first of many summer seminars in conjunction with the prestigious Lorian Association (a group that coalesced at Findhorn in the early 1970s). High Wind residents, along with seminar participants, join to pour the footings. Periodically visitors come to help complete the innovative structure that provides both living and classroom space, as well as becoming an important experiment of greenhouse horticulture. Showcasing a closed-loop growing system, the building is designed to actually produce, rather than consume, energy.

Participants in the first Lorian-High Wind summer seminar help pour concrete footings for the bioshelter foundation, Summer 1981.

Robert and Todd lay concrete block, 1981.

Jim (lead builder), Bel, an unidentified helper, and Tom hoist a beam into place, 1981.

Deep trusses allow for eighteen inches of insulation (R60) in the roof; Priscilla is one of our proficient carpenters, 1981.

David (in T-shirt), our technical coordinator, and a seminar participant install a wood stove, 1981.

Here we were, up in the country, grant in hand, just a few people living together in a ramshackle farmhouse and chicken coop to begin with, and a growing constituency of folks out there who wanted to support and align themselves with our dream. Such a strange, motley group we were: carpenters, professors, dolphin researchers, high techies, gardeners, human potential junkies, yoga practitioners, spiritual seekers, the emotionally fragile, writers. . . . But we began to do it. We carried concrete blocks and hoisted beams and Sheetrock, and slowly the bioshelter took shape. We planted our vegetables. We transferred many of the workshops that explored concepts about radical cultural change from Milwaukee to the farm. We managed somehow to feed and house these growing numbers who resonated with the ideas and flocked to our remote rural door for a shot of that grand vision of what could be for all society. The commodity in such short supply generally—a sense of purpose, of meaning in our lives—was being articulated at High Wind by this little crew, brave enough to drop everything else, including income production, to come and try to live the changes advocated.
— Lisa Paulson, "Love Letters to My Community," November 1989

Lisa (left) and Betsy roofing the bioshelter, 1982.

Marcia and I have been plastering and sanding in "the great hall" of the bioshelter. Instead of feeling driven by a seemingly endless chore, we get engrossed in throwing ideas back and forth while teetering on the tops of our ladders, gooping the ceiling. Then we stop to change the music tapes or try out a folk dance step we're learning. Or we drop our trowels and run out to the top of the hill to lie in the grass and watch the clouds for a while. Even a chronic workaholic like me can learn! And this is real joy. When work time and play time become blurred, the spirit sings and fatigue and heaviness fade.
— Lisa Paulson, Windwatch,
    September 1983

Completed bioshelter: greenhouse and residential space is on the left, meeting and more living space is on the right, 1995.

Reflections ON THE IDEA OF COMMUNITY FROM HIGH WIND RESIDENTS, PROGRAM LEADERS, AND PROGRAM PARTICIPANTS

I think the more people are willing to actively explore living the types of initiatives High Wind has undertaken, the more they will be able to expand their perspectives of life in this world. The broader your perspectives, the more compassion you will hopefully be able to manifest. And the more people experience the challenges inherent in living these visions daily, and don't throw in the towel, the better chance we have of having some impact on our culture.

There's always a gap between vision and reality. Those who come with particular expectations may become frustrated; if they expect complete freedom, they'll experience restriction; if seeking structure and direction, they may find themselves uncomfortably left to their own initiatives. . . . It goes without saying that societal transformation starts with individual well-being. People may come fired up about one and then will realize they need to embrace the other, too. Both are valued equally at High Wind, both are necessary. "Sustainable Development" gets back to discovering through small-scale trial and error experiments of micro-societies what really can work—human to human, human to environment.
— *Susan Newstead, program participant, 2005 High Wind Survey*

In community, all aspects of life are amplified. It is, on the one hand, a microcosm of society at large and, on the other hand, a macrocosm of the one-on-one interpersonal relationship. . . . Trying to understand the interrelatedness of all aspects—working to not stratify and compartmentalize the social, political, economic, philosophic, and spiritual aspects of existence as our occidental society is inherently inclined to do—this is the task, the goal, the necessity!
— *Etienne (Steve) Schuh, resident, from a paper*
written for the 1984 Three-Community Seminar

I'd like to see initiatives like High Wind grow now to a new level where the community is not just a geographic location but a mental/psychological one that people with similar interests and values could tie into no matter where they live.
— *Joy Decker, resident, 2005 High Wind Survey*

How could High Wind contribute to building a better world? By reaching a broader spectrum of the population. But will they come, or are they fearful of being co-opted?
— *Wil Kraegel, program leader, 2005 High Wind Survey*

High Wind is a part of a longer-term pioneering effort. I would love to see it use its experience and connections to seed collaborations between intellectual and established communities and new visionaries in its area of interest—spirituality and sustainability. Certainly the collective, cooperative nature of the new High Wind "neighborhood" is a model of collaborative stewardship. Your capacity to support other start-up initiatives with wisdom and seed money has wonderful impact potential.

— *Freya Secrest, program leader, 2005 High Wind Survey*

For all our progressive spirituality, we were not economically progressive. We seemed to hold ourselves above politics, above the substance of many critical social debates. . . . In a more general sense I think the problem was that we were mesmerized by the possibility that individualistic solutions might actually be able to address and even ameliorate social (and global) problems. . . . I like to blame the unfortunate and ubiquitous New Age mantra "you create your own reality" for this mistake. On the face of it, it is a hopeful belief, that individuals do not have to be victimized by the social world, and can take matters into their own hands. What gets left out is the fact that the social world has tremendous power over the lives of individuals, and this fact isn't erased by a mantra. Most people in the world do not have the resources to affect their own realities at all. If you are poor and uneducated and socially powerless, you need more than meditation to change your world.

We all had to go through what we all went through, because that's where we were then [in the late 1970s], that's who we were then, that's what our writers were writing, our thinkers were thinking, and our do-ers were doing. . . . We were so hopeful. I think we recognized all the positive signs in politics and culture as evidence that the New Age was upon us. . . . I wish we had been part of a social movement that had had more political and popular appeal. If I am honest, I have to say I didn't want that then. I wanted to retreat into utopia with other like-minded people. I wanted to work on myself and still feel I was making a positive contribution to the world. I see now that that was naïve, but I had to go through that time, to get me to this one."

— *Judith Pintar, program participant, 2005 High Wind Survey*

High Wind Workshops and Seminars

Many of the educational offerings begun in Milwaukee in 1977 move up to the country as High Wind facilities and staff are organized. There is a wide range of workshop topics—from renewable energy and other practical, hands-on technologies to philosophical/spiritual explorations and self-actualization techniques. Some take place over a weekend, others are spread out over one or two weeks. Some are led by our own residents—women's retreats, demonstrations of organic gardening, and alternative political think tanks—while others draw in noted leaders from across the country and abroad.

Sun Bear, famed Indian chief from the Pacific Northwest, draws 250, our biggest crowd.

We welcome other Indian medicine men and women and teachers of Native American culture; permaculture and ethnobotany experts; facilitators of Ira Progoff's Intensive Journal Workshop; originators of the Findhorn Game of Life; local and national politicians working for fundamental change of governance systems; solar architects; exemplars of various spiritual and esoteric paths; avant garde artists and musicians; and proponents of environmentally sensitive lifestyles.

Participants sleep in the bioshelter, barn, coop, the experimental Styrofoam/cement domes we erect, and in tents. Mostly High Wind residents prepare meals in the farmhouse and serve them in our dining room, the barn, or outside on the lawn.

Betsy, our first gardener (foreground), conducts an organic gardening workshop, 1982.

Findhorn founder Peter Caddy (dark sweater, center) at High Wind to lead a workshop, 1987.

Barbara (left) guides the Game of Life, 1987.

Joy and Bernadette labor in the kitchen with help from Anneke, 1989.

There are the eloquent thinkers, both resident and guest speakers, who have used High Wind as a forum. They have opened doors, planted seeds, and stretched my awareness. I learned that reading and listening are not enough, though.
— Mary Gnandt, resident, Windwatch, 1988

Sun Bear (in hat), famed native chief, draws 250 for his talk (Springdale Farm buildings in background), 1988.

Bil Becker gives a workshop on global ley lines
(natural energy convergences) at High Wind Books in
Milwaukee, 1987.

Communal art project: Waldorf education painting during
Learning Community retreat, 1992.

The first Women's Retreat,
held at High Wind in October
1986, filled quickly. Joann
Martens facilitated the group
with great sensitivity. We
walked the woods, moved
creatively, stretched our
psyches, danced at the fire
circle, and shared our stories.
I especially appreciated
the positive, upbeat quality
of the weekend, women
proudly standing in their
own space, not forgetting
 the pain of the past,
but moving beyond it.
— Barbara Prendergast (senior),
    program participant,
    Windwatch, April 1987

Joann Martens (facing camera, second from right) leads our first
women's retreat at Hawthorne House, 1986.

Indian Institute and Other Native American Activities

A strong impulse at High Wind is resonance with the venerable philosophy and worldview of Native American groups. We develop a relationship with local Wisconsin Ojibwe and Menomonee tribal leaders and craftspeople who come to share and teach their indigenous practices and skills. The two-week Indian Institute, led by eight native staff, is one of our most popular events. It emphasizes deep respect for the land, its gifts, and its unique healing qualities.

Lee Olsen prepares wood to make black ash baskets, 1982.

Jan Borgenhagen blesses Alida's newly bought land with a pipe ceremony in the fen, 1981.

Institute participants build a wigwam with branches we gather and bend, tied with "wikup" strips (the inner bark of soaked basswood).

John Boatman (Indian Institute director) at the bent oak tree, 1983.

John Boatman speaks about Ojibwe culture and philosophy, 1983.

John Boatman's lectures covered Indian village life and culture, the reality of dreams that link us to the spirit world, meanings in nature forms. . . . He also hypothesized that "our tree," a crooked black oak in the woods, was deliberately bent to mark an Indian council ground—over four hundred years ago.
— Lisa Paulson, reporting on the Indian Institute held at
    High Wind, Windwatch, September 1982

Drumming at the sacred fire circle.

Lee Olsen leads ethnobotany field walk, 1982.

Colleen Boatman and Harold Katchenago are married in our High Wind woods by a Menomonee medicine woman, 1983.

Living/Learning Seminars in Three Communities

In 1984, Bel arranges with the University of Wisconsin-Milwaukee to offer academic credit for a three-month course, sponsored with High Wind. It is the first of six Living Learning Seminars we organize, which draw participants from across North America to spend one month at High Wind, another at the Sirius community in Massachusetts or Eourres in the French Alps, and a third month at Findhorn in Scotland. Against the backdrop of these larger enclaves, the seminarians (twelve in the first experiment) create their own mini community.

It's an intense, exciting adventure that for most is life changing. In the final papers they write, the participants relate how unusual and rewarding it is to build a tight bond with the others in their little group where complete openness, vulnerability, and interdependence are essential. A leader/facilitator from High Wind accompanies each seminar, and each of the large communities designs a special program filled with rich experiences. Members of all the groups benefit from the heightened energy generated.

First Three-Community Seminar: tribe of "The Twelve" plus community member Pat Kiernan (top row, far right) at High Wind, 1984.

"The Twelve" plus community members Pat and Betsy Abert (standing at far right) at High Wind, the first of the three communities visited, 1984.

The Helios Café in Universal Hall at Findhorn is a busy social gathering hub for residents and visitors.

Some of our students eating outside the Findhorn community center.

For the first time in my life, I was in a community of like-minded people. I found spiritual guides and companions. I saw practical ways to build a sustainable life in the bioshelter (and later, in David's and the Paulsons' homes) and organic agriculture.
— Elizabeth Matson, program participant, 2005 High Wind Survey

1987 seminarians having dinner in the farmhouse with High Wind residents.

Marcia and Sheila, two of the students, are touched by a rainbow over Loch Ness, near Findhorn, 1984.

Transformation never ends. It is always in process: dying to ourselves, nurturing a new seed of inspiration, being accountable to it, watching it blossom, and letting it go again. A spiraling, a widening, a deepening. Ultimately transformation can only occur through relationship.

— *Sheila Morrow, Three-Community Seminar participant, Windwatch, September 1984*

Community at Work and Play

Early on, our all-consuming focus is the bioshelter—basically, we're a construction gang. Gradually educational events are incorporated into our busy schedule, because sharing the ideas, experiments, and everything we're learning is central to our purpose and is mandated by the grant.

Very soon we find ourselves grappling with the complexities of creating and maintaining a residential intentional community—managing logistics, work schedules, diet, interpersonal relationships, and feelings. Long meetings become a ubiquitous part of our regimen because all decisions are made by consensus. More and more people show up to join the community, and we settle into daily rounds that include hauling concrete block and wielding hammers, digging in the planting beds, slicing vegetables, greeting and briefing visitors, preparing spaces for workshops, running tours, putting out newsletters, instituting times for optional spiritual study and meditation, and organizing seasonal celebrations.

Bel hauls compost, 1989.

Don takes Bill's kids on a wild ride, 1991.

Lisa and Marcia, 1983.

Pat and Betsy (our first gardener) become a couple, 1984.

Earliest residents in
the farmhouse, 1982.
Clockwise from bottom center:
Alida, Bel, Cindy M.,
John, Lisa, Cindy S.,
Jim, and David.

Another most important reason for healthy plant growth was the joyous dedication of the gardeners. Often our work was begun with a quiet meditation in the garden that encouraged a gentle, aware approach. What those meditative moments offered me personally was the constant renewal and strengthening of the conviction that our goal is to create and build a balance and positive communication between ourselves and all of nature.
— *Betsy Abert, High Wind's first gardener, Windwatch, September 1981*

Alida digs French intensive raised vegetable beds with Joanne Lehman, 1981.

Residents and volunteers bless the first plantings, 1982.

John and Joann practice T'ai Chi, 1986.

Lorri (our second gardener) and her lettuces, 1983.

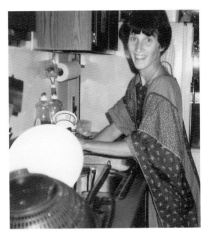

Lorri on kitchen duty.

In winter, Lorri dons another hat, now carpenter/painter, 1987.

It has been a perfect summer in the High Wind garden, as evidenced by over fifteen hundred pounds of organically-grown produce gathered. But the garden has provided us much, much more than food for our table. We're learning more about our relationship with Nature and gaining a deeper understanding and appreciation of the complex web of life. About sixty varieties of vegetables, herbs, and flowers were grown in the garden, which was expanded this year to approximately five thousand square feet of growing area. A grassy plot toward the center was turned into a "bird sanctuary," with feeders, baths and a martin house. . . . Interplantings of catnip and borage attracted huge numbers of honeybees, the latter playing an important part in pollination. Rock piles and watery areas bordering the garden provided habitat for beneficial garden snakes and toads. We welcome these creatures for their role in Nature's design. . . . The Earth has been a great teacher. . . . Our garden has become a special place, not only a place where we grow our vegetables, but a place where all forms of life are invited to participate in the co-creation and share the abundance. We honor the sacred relationships that exist here. There is a sense of celebration as the petals of a new blossom unfold because we know that we, too, are unfolding, and in that unfolding, our bodies and souls are nurtured.

— *Lorri Rhyner, High Wind gardener, Windwatch, October 1984*

Joann splits logs for the wood stoves, 1987.

After a tough month of struggling with bioshelter construction, we suddenly had to let go and concentrate on the more pressing priorities of coping with snow and cold. We began to function as a team once again and got into the yoga of starting and digging out the vehicles and chopping logs (our only heat is with a wood-burning furnace and three wood stoves). We were focusing outward, adjusting to the demands of the elements, listening to nature rather than our own circular arguments, and we discovered that the heaviness of difference melted away. The sun came out, along with the cross-country skis and tires for sliding down hills. Our moon boots squeaked more purposefully across the crystalline splendor, and we all felt a bit wiser.

— *Lisa Paulson*, Windwatch, *February 1982*

Residents in 1986. *Back row:* Lisa, Bel, Joann, and John; *front row:* Eric, Angelynn, Niko, Lark, David, Lorri, Etienne (Steve), Pam, and Jane.

Jane and Etienne create their nest in a corner of the barn, 1987.

Tiffany helps in the community kitchen, 1985.

Karina with the fall squash harvest, 1985.

Bel planting on the bioshelter terrace, 1985.

I helped keep the farmhouse clean and cooked one meal a week. I remember weeding in the garden, liquefying buckets and buckets of honey that had congealed, helping straighten up the place for events, cleaning out the barn and dairy shed, going through boxes of tomatoes and throwing out rotten ones. The biggest thing I did was run around barefoot all over the land.

— *Karina Martens, a teenager who came to live at High Wind with her mother, Joann Martens*

Betsy takes a break with her much loved Mike, 1985.

> I listened to Peter Caddy say you need to love what you're doing, love where you're doing it, and love who you're doing it with. It took me a year to understand and know what that meant.
> — *Mary Gnandt, as she left the community, Windwatch, Fall/Winter 1988*

David Lagerman relaxing in the farmhouse, 1990.

Residents in 1991. *Standing, from left:* Jan, Joyce, Ray, Don, Louise, Bill, Marcia, Walken, and David; *seated:* Lisa and Bel; *in front:* Bernadette, Anneke, Jimmy, and Peter.

Walken and Marcia under the apple blossoms, spring 1990.

Reflections ON THE CHALLENGES OF LIVING IN COMMUNITY FROM HIGH WIND RESIDENTS, PROGRAM LEADERS AND PROGRAM PARTICIPANTS

All of the comments below are taken from the 2005 High Wind Survey.

Deficiencies? There may have been too much community and perhaps not enough getting to task. High Wind seemed too loosely structured and spread itself too thin. It could have remained a social community but needed to let in others better. I felt it needed to think bigger—have bigger goals/plans/expectations.
— Pamm Steffen

We needed a clearer picture of where power and decision-making authority was held. [When I came] I was excited about the possibility of consensus decision-making and leadership. This was not happening here. In my way of looking at this, which is very personal, I think everyone here did the best they could with the knowledge they had of themselves at the time. If we can't find a new way of being together in small groups, peace in the world is not possible.
— Louise Mann

Community in this form requires a high level of commitment—to the work and to cooperation. It's something we Western, middle-class types were not raised up to be good at initially. . . . It's almost like being married to a group of people, which is good in some ways, of course. The dynamics get complicated, though.

As for how the community functioned, this was probably, in hindsight, our weakest element. There was no strong leadership (by design), which meant we often lacked focus. Things got out of hand, which led the Paulsons to do the right thing: set up a board of directors and appoint the initial board. Throughout, decision-making was by consensus, which doesn't work well. Most often, we failed to "sound a clear note," as the Findhorn saying goes.

We generally lacked any kind of rigorous training in spiritual, philosophical, technical, or administrative fields, and were navigating by the seat of our pants. Does it matter? Yes and no. We did a lot. We learned a lot.
— David Lagerman

I was always very attuned to High Wind's environmental goals, and indeed invested many, many thousands of dollars (lost them) and a marriage (lost it) over the Silver Springs/Plymouth Institute adventure. Ultimately it began to consume every aspect of my life . . . and I couldn't continue participation. There was literally no room for my own work, dreams, or intuitions. . . .
— Bethe Hagens

There was too much emphasis on those who lived on the land. High Wind might have engaged the Associates [in the city] and formed a solid base of people who were not so likely to move on. My experience at High Wind has shown me that there are a lot of people who care about others and the land and generally want to be a part of the solution. Actually, much in what could be called "the New Age" has been beneficial to society.

— *Barbara Prendergast (senior)*

Having stepped away from the community, I can see more clearly the underlying problems and needs. And I can view with mellowed eyes the dysfunctions and discords we lived with—such as why people "tweaked" on each other and felt burned out or otherwise too overwhelmed and immobilized to stay on task.

— *Joy Decker*

I found it hard to work with extreme liberals who were nature conservatives. There was too much idealism. I guess there's a fine line between dictatorship and consensus. High Wind was too much into consensus. . . . What do I think High Wind was about? Holding a space in the collective consciousness for man's upcoming expressions. . . . Impact on the mainstream? It's not cause and effect that makes a difference in mainstream society. I'm sure the power of High Wind's intention has greatly affected society through a field of consciousness in ways beyond my understanding.

— *Jim Kennard*

What I've taken away from my experience with High Wind is that good people with good intentions can do good things—and good people with good intentions can make mistakes. . . . I love and respect you all. I hope the High Wind experiment and community, in whatever form, will go on forever.

— *Alan Zuberbuehler*

I lived at High Wind from age thirteen to sixteen. I am a person who has been privileged to have a rich spiritual and creative life. High Wind aided this development by acting as a cradle. It was a place where I could live out my late adolescence away from the noise caused by the endless social pounding of the hammers of consumerism. . . . I don't think for me there were any downsides of living in community. Because I came as the kid of a member, just sort of along for the ride, I got to enjoy the pluses, but then I had the unique privilege of letting the negatives— endless meetings, finance troubles, differences in vision, adult interpersonal conflicts, etc.—just float past me.

— *Karina Martens*

Chapter Five

Challenges and Achievements

Sometimes I think the tensions and problems and complexities we live with constantly at High Wind are close to unbearable, and then I come back to the city and see people mechanically watching television or trying to decide where to go out for dinner—the "walking dead"—and I realize how alive I am!

— *David Lagerman, High Wind resident, April 1985*

It is not surprising that when a group of intensely dedicated individuals live and work in close quarters there are both serious conflicts and dazzling successes. This was certainly the case with High Wind.

THE DARKER SIDE

How communities struggle with negativity and conflict is often what outsiders are most curious about. So to counterbalance the positive face we showed most often, I want to lay out here, as honestly as possible, some of the more challenging issues and feelings we had to deal with.

Power and Control:
Founders in the Hot Seat

In our early years, 1981-83, when the very core of High Wind's purpose was dedication to equality, Bel and I were genuinely surprised to suddenly have to defend ourselves against accusations of being too dominant. The residents attacked us for contradicting our own rhetoric. Despite our strenuous denial,

it was obvious they felt we *were* too powerful. They complained that we took advantage of our position to manipulate and control decisions, and they said that nothing ever happened if we weren't in favor of it. At one point, Jim Priest said, "It doesn't matter what the Paulsons say or do; just their *existence* puts pressure on everyone. It feels like Big Brother looking over our shoulder." He pointed out that we were the founders, we owned most of the land, and I put my own spin on High Wind and its activities and people by writing articles on these subjects in *Windwatch*. Clearly this *did* make us powerful and also made us the High Wind "parents." There was a tendency for those not holding power to criticize those they thought *did* have the power.

On the other hand, our Lorian friends kept telling us we needed to exercise *stronger* leadership, not to be so "democratic." If our goal was to create an alternative to mainstream culture, we needed to keep our vision and purpose crystal clear. They said High Wind represented a "myth" that people were latching onto; it was where one could go to take a stand.

We discovered that those who came from dysfunctional families, or who hadn't yet resolved their own parent/child relationships, were looking for surrogate parents, and this is what Bel and I (a generation older than some of them) represented. And, like most adolescents, they tended to rebel against whomever they perceived to be authority figures. Maybe there was an inability (or refusal) to discern power-over as distinct from power-with.

As the community "parents," Bel and I often became scapegoats for members' frustrations. As resident "vision-holder," I was nailed for writing what they saw as "rhetoric" that sometimes masked a less positive reality. Also, I came across to them as overly romantic, tending to write or speak "colorfully," dramatizing or exaggerating to make a point. The community would take this literally and then be irritated to find that I was just being "poetic." I preferred to fall back on a quote on my wall by the painter Matisse: "Exactitude is not the truth."

Sometimes Bel and I felt unwelcome in our own community; we were criticized as "city people," and those toughing it out at the farm fell naturally into what they saw as their own proud little closed enclave. Often visitors felt shut out as well.

When attending a gathering of intentional communities from around the world at Findhorn in 1982, we heard the same war stories from leaders of other communities. They all suffered "Founders' Fatigue" from taking primary responsibility for holding the energy in their groups. They all had the same power and money problems. And everyone seemed to be moving toward more decentralization in an effort to defuse the tensions that invariably built up when members became so closely entwined. Of course, this contradicts the reason people seek community in the first place—because we live in a culture where there's *too much* isolation. It's an interesting paradox that the community movement addresses.

> From a thin-skinned person whose sense of worth depended on people loving me, I stoically decided it was true that founders and leaders of groups like ours were seldom liked. They were the lightning rods for the self-hatred of others, the object of projection, the parent figures to rebel against.
>
> — Lisa Paulson, from diary notes, June 1993

More Community Issues

Sometimes I was challenged for being unclear, for not coming out directly to say what was bothering me because I didn't want to hurt or offend people, and also because I didn't want to be disliked. In some ways, I was too "thin-skinned" for this job. On the other hand, Bel was faulted for being "thick-skinned," for not being sensitive enough; his eye was usually on the larger picture, not so much on the consequences for individuals. (After college, he had worked in the waterfront slums of Naples, Italy, where survival required a certain imperviousness or thick skin in the face of appalling conditions.) He was more comfortable focusing on projects than relationships. In meetings, some frustrated members pushed everyone to share their intimate feelings. "I want to feel your pain," they said. Bel, like many men in our society, balked at this intrusion on his privacy, saying he didn't have any pain—which people either didn't believe or thought he was just insensitive. Either way he couldn't win.

Specific issues could turn thorny. For instance, Betsy lobbied to keep the door between the farmhouse living room and the greenhouse open on cold winter nights so her tomatoes and lettuce wouldn't freeze. The strict conservationists ganged up, howling about the inexcusable heat loss the house was suffering. She gave up and let the plants die, but it was painful for her to lose everything she'd nurtured for months.

We also noted an ongoing blame game. Generally when *everyone* was supposed to be responsible for a job (or tools), it turned out that *no one* took responsibility; tools were misplaced or rusted out, projects neglected. This often happened just because members had different habits or standards, but invariably somebody would start pointing a self-righteous finger. We saw how this mindset changed completely when individuals had a personal stake in an operation—the perfect example being when Peter and Bernadette Seely later bought and took control of Springdale, the lower farm, as a private business.

As these issues came up, in the moment each loomed as a crisis. Only much later could we see them as "growth opportunities" and could agree that they'd made us stronger.

The Haves and Have-Nots

Early on, we saw a problem of perceived hierarchy developing. Everyone was supposed to be equal within the community, but some members were more skilled and naturally fell into more high-level work, while others began to see themselves as stuck in "grunt" jobs. Bosses versus grunts; home owners versus volunteers who lived in the public buildings. Some people expressed feelings of powerlessness and disenfranchisement, and resented the exercising of power, not just by Bel and me but by one group over another.

When the question came up of some people wanting to build houses on the hill, others objected immediately. This would result in a class system within the community, they said—those with money and those without, those owning private property and those who could never afford it. They warned of an increasing separation of these factions. Later (after our Lorian friends applauded the idea of a permanent village on the ridge), one of the first to start building said he was thankful Bel and I still had power. (We owned all the High Wind land except the acre for the bioshelter and the land and buildings we donated for the "campus,"

> Any limitations have been merely the reflections of the limitations we had in wherever our spiritual maturity was at any given time. I don't feel High Wind could have done anything differently—it did the best it could throughout its journey.
>
> We, as participants in the process, may have felt disappointment and held judgments on others and ourselves, but in the end it was all perfect.
>
> — Joann Martens , *High Wind resident, 2005 High Wind Survey*

although, in effect, we had turned over the whole property for High Wind use.) He said we were being manipulated by "the squatters."

WITH FRESH WAVES OF RESIDENTS, IT'S DÉJÀ VU

All these tensions surfaced before 1984. After this, some of the earlier crew moved on, and with the new influx, there was a fresh dedication to building our spiritual life, seeing High Wind as a center that was part of a "great network of light." In general, the community did indeed begin to feel a lot lighter; we felt we were flying! We were sure we'd turned a corner.

But then, by 1986, we were into our "third wave," and those who had come just a couple of years before were, themselves, starting to burn out. Negativity crept back over us.

Two of our strongest leaders, Joann Martens and John Reeves, announced that the very *thought form* of High Wind was oppressive: the image (that they'd helped to craft) of our global/holistic mission, our perceived significance, our bigness (as we acquired more land and buildings). With our growing commitments to programming, servicing guests, and expansion in all ways, they were beginning to feel a constant heaviness and anxiety; the fun had gone out of the enterprise. The tranquility we advertised and provided for visitors was eluding those of us on the ground holding it all together.

> At High Wind, those who influenced me most were Bel and Lisa because they provided leadership and were fearless; because they bridged High Wind and the university; because they took risks; because they balanced intuition and mind.
>
> — *Milenko Matanovic, Lorian Leader, 2005 High Wind Survey*

A new member complained that there was no mechanism for individuals with creative ideas and energy to carry out their own inspired schemes. She felt that because everything had to be decided by everyone, the process was just too clumsy. "It's the contrived togetherness we impose on each other that gets me down most," she said.

The old dichotomy between the "doers" and the "processors" loomed sharply again. The processors wanted to spend hours and hours sorting out inner personal dynamics and reflecting on our collective psyche. The action folks got very impatient with this use of precious time.

The gap between the vision and reality resurfaced and was pointed out. Bel noted that, yes, this was indeed true, but wasn't it always the case in life? He agreed we *were* raising expectations. If people were drawn here, they needed to realize *they* were High Wind and were taking on responsibility equal to the founders and the other residents. (People were again feeling Bel and I were laying our expectations on everyone else.) At that point, we had to stop in our tracks and recognize that personality issues usually did trump practical decisions.

When we first bought the sixty-two-acre complex next to High Wind, a growing disconnect developed between the group going to live there and the folks living on the main campus. Feelings of separation became acute, exacerbated by the fact that the two groups divided along lines of very different personalities. The lower farm faction focused on agricultural activities—raising animals and getting the fields planted. They were nuts-and-bolts types and saw their efforts as more "real world" perhaps than the idealists on the ridge. The latter faction concentrated on the "higher" or "global mission," which meant outreach and offering services to visitors, our wider High Wind Associates (supporters), and workshop goers. It meant being on call continually to interact with the public.

Sometimes we had a tendency to start a project with great enthusiasm and then not carry it through. People jumped in to give it their full energy, but then a newer idea would come along and the leadership would leap to the fresher fields, leaving the first group dangling without support. The glamorous focal point had shifted.

We found we *could* implement and exemplify the ideology of High Wind, but only in spurts. People were bound to burn out; for all sorts of reasons they became frustrated, or even bitter, and left. We saw we were "chewing people up." At one point, a dramatic meeting was called where a mediator asked members to form clusters around the future direction they'd choose for the community: "fundamental change" or "make what exists work." (I went with the former, Bel the latter, and the rest of the group was pretty evenly split.)

> I was never resentful or disillusioned. I was disappointed that the effort didn't continue to thrive, but that was such a long shot that I don't entertain any regrets about anything. We were just *ordinary people*, and though we differed from one another, we shared a commitment to make things better and tried really hard. I am proud to have been a part of this.
>
> — *David Lagerman, High Wind resident, 2005 High Wind Survey*

By the latter 1980s, Bel had concluded that our commitment to the residential element was perhaps less significant than our commitment to consciousness. He was disenchanted with the residential community, with all of its logistic problems, psychological snares, and ego traps. He felt what we were really proving and exemplifying was a shift in consciousness, a commitment to new ways of seeing the world, and our purpose—the deeper underlying reason we were here—contrasted with the picayune issues that often sabotaged our moving forward smoothly.

In 2005, we circulated a lengthy questionnaire to our current residents, former members, and supporters. We asked them, in retrospect, how they would characterize High Wind. One resident remarked, "We were a bunch of dysfunctional people trying to make a difference." (Touché!)

Some came to High Wind expecting to be taken care of, both physically and emotionally. They generally went through the classic stages: there was bubbly idealism at first—the "honeymoon period," then dark disillusion, and, finally, a leveling-off where they saw that, after all, communities are simply made up of people leading "divinely ordinary lives" (as they liked to say at Findhorn).

These, then, are some of the potential hazards of choosing to live in community or—maybe even more risky—deciding to start or lead a community. Sometimes we viewed all the "sanding off of rough corners" as an important therapeutic exercise, though of course each of us at times felt a victim of the harsh judges or circumstances around us. What needs to be recognized is that we were fully as "human" as people anywhere, but we were choosing to learn (or were made to learn) to be more aware of our blind spots. And despite the negative tales detailed above, most of us "came out the other side," saw the rewards, and eventually were deeply appreciative of our experiences and of the commitment we'd made to work for change on all levels.

WHERE EVERYBODY LIVED

Initially most of the residents stayed in the farmhouse, dubbed the "pressure cooker" because it became pretty intense with people from every sort of background crowded into one building. Then, gradually, we began to decentralize. Residents realized if they were going to be here for a while, in order not to burn out, they needed more privacy, space to spread out and regain a sense of creative autonomy. They carved out rooms in the barn, the restored chicken coop, and the bioshelter. Along the way, when a few members had bought land (from Bel and me) to build their own houses, we explored the idea of forming a community land trust. We believed in the idea that no one should own land, any more than one could possess the moon or stars, and that land should be protected forever. But some who had put down deep roots were afraid of someday losing the considerable

sums they'd already invested in their homes, and we dropped the plan.

Bel and I had continued to keep our main residence in Milwaukee because of Bel's heavy university responsibilities, though we always held a room in the farmhouse and spent weekends and large blocks of time in the country. It was with the greatest delight, therefore, when the time came in 1985 when we felt we could begin building our own home at High Wind. At last, we would feel an integral part of the community we had founded. We worked meticulously to design a state-of-the-art passive solar structure where energy consumption was cut drastically, and where conservation features and practices could be demonstrated for the thousands of visitors who would come to tour the community.

It was particularly important for me to show that a technologically correct solar house could be aesthetically attractive. This was achieved largely with the help of a sensitive carpenter friend, Keith Symon, who had gone on one of our Findhorn seminars and was an expert on solar design. I served as general contractor, working closely with Keith and Pete Paiser, a local builder and specialist in earth-sheltered homes. I was on hand nearly every day during the nine months of construction to eyeball the progress, help decide changes on the spot, and line up subcontractors.

The house, being next to the woods and protected on the north, is dug into the west hill so that roughly half the building is underground, sheltered from the prevailing winter west winds. The other half of the house is passive solar and super insulated, exposed to capture the sun and sweeping views over the valley on the east and south. From the beginning, the architecture was dictated by the land, with the house growing organically out of the existing earth contours and giving a feeling of stepping down with the hill. The interior spaces evolved out of this natural flow and from light patterns from the huge triple-glazed windows. An air-to-air heat exchanger continually flushes out stale air and brings in the fresh. Much of our hot water is supplied by active solar panels. We decided to call our new home Hawthorne House; each spring the hedgerow of tangled wild hawthorne trees on our east border becomes a cloud of white blossoms.

Our son, Eric, and Angelynn Brown had married in 1980, having met and fallen in love while Angelynn was living with us in Milwaukee. (My best friend and colleague became my daughter-in-law!) The two of them (and their newborn daughter Lark) lived briefly in our farmhouse before the community took it over. A few months later, they moved to Madison, but in 1986 (now with two small kids), they were back at High Wind to help us build our new home. They had planned to live in a tent in our yard, but then saw they might make a contribution to the community and moved into the bioshelter. (Eric is a landscaper/builder.) They left High Wind when they felt that their rather advanced and independent ideas were not being heard by the community. They also had felt a strong need to establish an identity as a family unit apart from a group setting. Although they had lived at High

Wind for only six months, Eric came back several times to develop the landscaping, to build a solar addition to the farmhouse, and to create the boardwalks down in the fen.

As our programs grew, we needed more space for guests, so Jim Priest and David Lagerman designed and built three innovative domes. These were low-cost structures of twelve-inch-thick Styrofoam blocks glued together, covered with cement mixed with fiberglass, and then covered with a waterproof coating. Such "cement igloos" were definitely an improvement over guests' tents, which often flooded. There was also a very effective solar shower that relieved pressure on our single bathroom in the farmhouse.

BUILDING ON OUR EDUCATION CORNERSTONE: SHARING EXPERIENCES, IDEAS, AND VALUES

The highlight of each summer season for nearly twenty years was when some or all of our good Lorian friends—David and Julie Spangler, Myrtle Glines, Milenko and Kathi Matanovic, Katherine and Roger Collis, Dorothy Maclean, and Freya Secrest—came for a one- or two-week gathering at High Wind. Mornings we sat in the huge barn—with sunlight dancing off the high rough beams and pigeons cooing in the silo—to pinpoint all the dire planetary challenges and then to envision not only immediate practical solutions but ideal long-range possibilities for our culture.

Afternoons were for work projects (where serious conversations continued), walks in the woods, and ferocious volleyball games. In the evenings we might have more sharing of ideas or zany skits parodying the woes of the world, or spoofing each other and the over-earnestness of the community movement or "New Age" (of which we had to admit we were probably a part, though it was a pariah term we painstakingly avoided). Sometimes we tramped off for a night hike through the forest, guided by a full moon, or chased fireflies along the spine of our country road with mists rolling off to either side. Or we spread blankets at the sacred fire circle to sing or watch the northern lights.

Preceding one of our gatherings, David Spangler summed up our task in honoring the paradigm shift required in this new era: "The modern quest for an understanding and practice of an attitude of wholeness that can transcend and heal the confrontations of our fragmented world and lives is a spiritual adventure. It is a rediscovery of the sacredness of ourselves, of our world and of our relationships. . . . We seek to demonstrate that spirituality is more than a religious term or idea; it is a vision of a quality of life and relationship inherent as a creative and unifying potential in everything we do."

Milenko Matanovic spoke often of what's missing in the dominant culture that people are yearning for: small scale and connectedness—the major reasons for starting or joining communities.

> High Wind was a righteous place that served as a beacon, a haven, a way station. I have no doubt that the community and the organization was a powerful positive influence on many people, just as it was for me. I would not be who I am without the years I spent as part of the High Wind circle of folks.
>
> — *Judith Pintar, High Wind program participant, 2005 High Wind Survey*

Seminar participants could get a beguiling taste of both in their time at these gatherings.

Futurist economist Robert Theobald, who gave a workshop for us in Milwaukee, offered this analogy of what's starting to happen: mainstream society is on a railroad train stuck on one track, rushing toward a precipice. New groups sense the emergency and see themselves as scouts or guerrillas, able to move with flexibility and speed. They get on a helicopter from which they can see ahead and maneuver freely; they're not going to get stuck on the tracks going over the cliff.

WHAT DO COMMUNITIES OFFER? PROS AND CONS

Generally the intentional communities of today are more mature than those that opted out of the mainstream in the 1960s and 1970s and are certainly more balanced than the utopians of the mid-nineteenth century. The current enclaves see themselves as little R&D stations—laboratories where new values and ways of living can be tried out on a manageable scale. Later, in the 1980s, the United Nations began to call this approach "sustainability"—the holistic aggregate of issues concerning resources, land, and civilization, taking care of today's needs without compromising the needs of future generations. Now the term is widely accepted and understood, but in our early years it was rarefied jargon.

How many people wander aimlessly, forever seeking their identity, something to believe in, to belong to? Discovering others on the same path is a great gift for communitarians. For many it also becomes a path from which there is no return. It means acquiring an identity that may follow them for the rest of their lives.

There can be a downside to being identified with particular beliefs that are out of synch with the prevailing attitudes. This may be especially true when the beliefs represent a global consciousness that is trying to step away from the arrogance and avarice of parochial societies. Anyone who has been part of such an avant-garde group has sometimes felt the sting, the loneliness, and the sense of entrapment in an idea or label that follows one around.

At High Wind, we've been surprised by (or have smiled at) rumors that rippled out in our small conservative town: when simply burning trash became a "satanic ritual" (supposedly we were "dancing around a fire in black robes"); or when hunters I encountered in the nearby state forest asked where we kept our animals for sacrifice; or when drumming around a fire at our Indian Institute "proved" we were a dangerous cult. In fact, anyone *not* living in a conventional nuclear family and raising Holstein cows on eighty acres and showing up at a local church on Sunday could be suspect.

Meetings, Meetings, and More Meetings

A lot of sticky issues come unglued between meetings. If it takes longer, we wait. Our patience seems to stem from our awareness that our process is more important than our results and that we must each be comfortable with decisions if they are to work. . . . Whatever else this "New Age" may be, it is a human network in which sharing and trust take the place of competition. We seem to have been drawn to High Wind to prepare for and experience this. When a conflict arises, there is an automatic tendency to look within, to see how we need to grow to encompass the other's point of view. . . . Somehow the High Wind spirit, the dream that drew us all here, is pulling for us. The success of our somewhat haphazard decision-making process has made us aware of the power and safety that come from a dedication to the common good.

— *Alida Sherman, High Wind resident,*
Windwatch, *Fall/Winter, 1981*

Community meeting in the big dome, 1985. *Left to right:* Joann, Karina, Etienne, Jane, Bel, and Betsy.

Marcia facilitates the Game of Life to help us decide future directions, 1992.

Residents and board members at a heavy-duty retreat at Don Austin's cabin in northern Wisconsin, 1988.

Community meeting in the farmhouse, 1991.

We are willing to "wrap our tails around the branch" and stay with a deeply felt disagreement until we can come to a consensus answering the concerns of every person.
— *Jan Christensen, discussing what it's like to live and work in "the fishbowl," Windwatch, Spring/Summer 1990*

A limitation of High Wind was its difficulty in integrating personal vision with collective effort.
— *Freya Secrest, High Wind program leader, 2005 High Wind Survey*

Some meetings are one-on-one: Milenko and David L. confer over lunch.

Residents work through thorny issues with outside mediator/counselor David Thome (on right), 1990.

Mediator Donna Thome leads meditation following an intense meeting, 1990.

It is here that I am working out my "I have to sit through meetings" karma. Group decision-making requires processing a multitude of options, variables, and disagreements while arriving at a general consensus. I never knew that getting from point A to B could have so many points in between. I am learning patience. I am learning how it is fear that divides us while love unites us.
— Mary Gnandt, resident, Windwatch, April 1987

Looking back on it, my time at High Wind was a grace-filled period loaded with learning. An important concept I've taken from my High Wind experience: valuing everyone's contribution in a situation regardless of whether or not I'm in agreement.
— Joann Martens, resident, 2005 High Wind Survey

Private Enterprise at High Wind

In order to support themselves economically, and because High Wind cannot pay them, residents dip into slim savings. Eventually some must find part-time work outside the community. Others fear this would defeat their purpose; they are here for total immersion into an alternative lifestyle situation of living simply, sustainably, and responsibly, in close cooperation with nature and others who are sharing a similar path.

A few residents begin to carve out income-producing enterprises on site. Scattered around the property that has now expanded to include an additional set of farm buildings next door, we find furniture-making; desktop publishing; and woven fabrics, candles and other art products in a shop in the bioshelter. In the late 1980s, members Peter and Bernadette Seely buy the "lower farm" (Springdale) and create what is reportedly the first CSA in the Midwest—a highly successful natural farming subscription operation that feeds over six hundred families in the region. We find that bartering goods and services among ourselves also works well (e.g. exchanging tailoring a shirt in return for figuring income taxes).

Marcia at her loom; she opens a shop at High Wind with her weavings, also including candles and artwork, 1983.

Mary measures John for a new shirt, one of many barter transactions among community members, 1986.

Rick and Mary and two of their boys focus on raising animals at Springdale, High Wind's lower farm, 1987.

Don creates a furniture-making business in a barn at Springdale, 1989.

Rick in the workshop, making futons and benches with Don, 1987.

Jan brings desktop publishing expertise to High Wind; she goes into business with Louise in the dome she built, 1992.

It seems to me we all need to question ourselves; how much do we really need? Is that need sustainable for the planet and ourselves? If David and I decide to expand our home, am I willing to work at a high paying but not fulfilling job for a few years to pay for it? How does my need impact the earth? If I commute fifty miles a day to get to my job, what are the consequences to the air, to the infrastructure, to the car, to my nerves? If I decide to work part-time and spend the "leftover" time in meditation, music, reading, and sharing, will I be able to make enough money to live? In talking to many people in my parents' generation, they *knew* the years of work they had put in to provide security for their families and their own retirement left scars on their bodies and in their minds. Must I do this as well? Can't we as a society find a better way to live, a more humane structure?
— Louise Mann, resident, Windwatch, *Spring/Summer 1990*

Bernadette and Peter, with Anneke, pick vegetables in the lower fields; later they buy Springdale Farm from High Wind, 1988.

Bernadette waters seedlings in one of several greenhouses at Springdale, 1990.

Anneke and Jimmy at Springdale, 1990.

I've always regretted that we couldn't get a cottage industry going so that High Wind itself could be sustainable—sustainability for the community with its values and premises, and for the people who tried to embody and promote them.
— Joy Decker, resident, 2005 High Wind Survey

The Next High Wind Buildings and Lands—
Some Private and Some Owned by the High Wind Association

In the mid-1980s, some of the residents realize that what is unfolding in the community is deeply meaningful, and are ready to commit to the next step. They want to put down roots at High Wind and build a permanent home, which will be an important demonstration of appropriate technology. They are eager to work on the goals of the Association for the long haul. Bel and I agree to sell one-acre lots on the ridge to David Lagerman and to Don Mueller with his partner Joyce Hahn. We select a parcel for ourselves next to the woods. At first there is strenuous disapproval from a few members who feel this would

split the community into "haves" and "have-nots." Then friends who have experienced similar situations convince us that it is important to establish the solidity of long-term supporters. Those in our public buildings tend to come and go and aren't necessarily thinking in terms of being here into the foreseeable future.

Don and Joyce begin building the first private solar home in 1985, next to the bioshelter. Along the way, we tuck a tiny, primitive hermitage into the woods. Our three previously constructed Styrofoam/cement domes continue to serve as sleeping facilities for guests and members, and as meditation space.

Don Mueller and Joyce Hahn's home: the first of the private solar residences on the ridge, 1985.

Hermitage in the woods is built by John Reeves and Don Austin with Three-Community Seminar students, 1986.

Bel and I are next. One of my goals is to create a house that not only showcases state-of-the-art energy saving technologies, but is also aesthetically compelling. I want to prove that it isn't necessary to sacrifice beauty for efficiency.

David, our hands-on technical expert, breaks ground for his house in 1987, and after contracting out the foundation and framing, takes over to finish the house himself, now shared with his wife Louise. In 1990, Jan Christensen purchases her acre and erects a geodesic dome for herself and her young daughter.

At first, we call the new houses on the ridge "the ecovillage," but soon realize that this is probably pretentious; now we think of ourselves simply as an "eco-neighborhood."

Bel and I had previously donated the acre for the bioshelter and had deeded the farmhouse/barn complex to High Wind. Residents and visitors have always had access to all the land the community or individuals own.

Twenty acres west of the farmhouse are added when a group of our supporters join together to buy the land to save it from developers. With the sixty-two acres, including Springdale Farm to our east, the High Wind lands total 128 acres.

David Lagerman and Louise Mann's Photon House, 1987.

Jan Christensen's geodesic dome, 1990.

Hawthorne House

Coming out of our third winter at Hawthorne House, the home Bel and I finally built at High Wind, I continue to be amazed at how we have to strip down to T-shirts when the sun blazes through our Heat Mirror windows, even in the coldest weather. One of the really satisfying things about living in a passive solar house is looking out at mountains of snow glinting under a brilliant sky. It's February and below zero out there, but in my living room it's 80 degrees. Also satisfying is knowing I'm not using any wood in my stove, and I don't need (or have) central heating as backup. I won't have to light fires later, either, because heat is being stored in the slate floors and hearthstones, and will slowly release during the night. There are no fans or machines to make this happen; the house just sits there and performs its silent magic.

— *Lisa Paulson, describing her solar house at High Wind*, Windwatch, *Spring/Summer 1989*

Hawthorne House interior, 1995. (Photograph courtesy of Eric Oxendorf.)

Getting in the winter wood supply, 1988.

Lisa and Bel outside Hawthorne House, their solar home, 1995. (Photograph by Ronald M. Overdahl, reproduced by permission of the *Milwaukee Journal.*)

Lorian Workshops and Seminars

In 1977, the high-powered Lorian Association arrives in Milwaukee. Lorian had been key to conceiving and developing the educational thrust at Findhorn. Author and philosopher David Spangler is sometimes called "the father of the New Age." (In that era there were starry-eyed admirers who imagined him as something akin to the "Second Coming;" some, at the other extreme, feared he might be the Antichrist. To those of us who got to know him well, though, he was quite human: loveable, wise, an incurable punster—and played a killer game of Monopoly.) David and Milenko Matanovic, a Yugoslav musician and artist, with four others of their group, had been looking for a base since returning from Findhorn in 1973. After meeting Bel at a couple of our workshops, they decide to accept his invitation to settle for a while in the Midwest.

For much of his life, David has lived in the far-out realm of esoteric/cosmic questions and influences. He sees that combining this background with Bel's opposite experience in meeting economic, political, and social problems on the ground is exactly what could benefit both of them if they were to teach together. A balanced understanding of how these two worlds urgently need each other could lead to a new cultural synthesis, new approaches to resolving problems in our often polarized society.

Bel arranges for the University of Wisconsin-Milwaukee to hire David and Milenko as ad hoc faculty. By now they are well known locally as well as worldwide for their writings, music recordings,

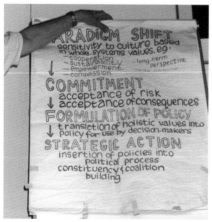

Props abound for the many weighty topics addressed.

Morning lectures and discussions in High Wind's venerable barn.

and concerts (and Findhorn connection). They and their group become a powerful magnet at the nonstop seminars, national conferences, and weekend workshops we organize. Because of the frequent spiritual (if broadly eclectic) overtones in their teaching, Bel must be circumspect in how he describes course offerings in the catalogs of a public university.

All this is unfolding just as High Wind is struggling to be born. Having been leaders in formulating Findhorn's early direction, Milenko and David are extraordinarily insightful in guiding us through tricky shoals in our own formative first years.

While continuing to teach classes in Milwaukee, the Lorian crew happily agrees to participate in what becomes the highly anticipated, ongoing, annual event up at High Wind—our joint Lorian-High Wind-university summer seminars.

From 1981 into the early 1990s, we attract participants of all ages from across the U.S. to live in our rustic environment for one or two weeks. Here they get a taste of community: mornings for philosophical dialogue around the theme of the particular seminar; afternoons jumping into physical work projects and relaxing in the lovely, natural ambience; and evenings for more informal discussion, skits, music, folk dancing, or partying.

One example of a seminar theme: "The Inner Dimensions of a Sustainable Culture, Working Through the Clash of Cosmologies, and Transcending the Conflict Between the Spiritual Image of Limitlessness and the Ecological Need for Limits."

In 1998, nearly one hundred alumni of collective explorations with Lorian return to High Wind for a twentieth anniversary celebration.

Bel leads a discussion.

David Spangler and Milenko Matanovic are the Lorian spearheads; here David holds forth in the bioshelter.

A talk on the High Wind lawn with David Spangler.

Dorothy Maclean (one of Findhorn's three founders, now with Lorian) gives a talk in the barn. (Photograph by Tim Conner.)

David Spangler had a great influence on me. I saw a grounded sacredness to life, not spiritual matters removed from life. . . . I see High Wind now as more practical than I used to. I had gone looking for a "retreat" to spirituality, but they brought spirituality to the real world issues. Lisa has also affected me as a strong role model for women today.
— Susan Safran, program participant, 2005 High Wind Survey

Breakout discussion: Lorians Dorothy (on left), and Myrtle Glines (sitting in chair).

Dorothy, the "deva lady," weeds in our garden.

David meets Louise at a Lorian seminar; in 1989 they become the new couple.

Staff meeting during a summer seminar. *Clockwise from left:* Bel, John, Milenko, Julie Spangler, Michael Lindfield (formerly at Findhorn), David Spangler, and Corinne McLaughlin (Sirius cofounder).

Circle dance in the yard. (Photograph courtesy of Tim Conner.)

Folk dancing behind the coop.

Milenko makes music at a Hawthorne House party.

Afternoon work project: Lois shows her strength moving a huge rock; David Somsky helps.

Macho guys . . .

Bel orchestrates the annual beer and bratwurst cookout. (This is the one meal during the year when we ditch our vegetarian diet.)

. . . and equally assertive women.

Looking back, High Wind brought in the voice of "practical application" that I carry with me now.
— *Freya Secrest, Lorian program leader, 2005 High Wind Survey*

"Attunement" before lunch gets rowdy as we practice levitation.

Blessing dance—Jim and Milenko.

Testing the new dock built by Lorian participants.

Seminar participants climb our aged silo in a silly moment.

Lisa with the two Barbara Prendergasts.

Lunch on the lawn.

Volleyball or soccer at any hour.

What I gained from my association with High Wind was mostly inspiration and a sense that there are other thoughtful people struggling with the same issues that had, and largely still have, my attention. . . . High Wind does seem to maintain a balance between talking and doing, thinking and acting. Too often educational structures are content with the accumulation of what they call knowledge and have no genuine interest in actually solving problems or lifting humanity. I think on the whole the focus has been to take ideas into the world and test them there rather than in the contrived laboratories of institutions.

— *John Weaver, program participant, 2005 High Wind Survey*

Break time chats.

Betsy and George entertain the troops after a cookout.

The entire Lorian crew returns for the 1998 Twentieth Anniversary Reunion: *From left to right:* Milenko, Lara, Roger, Katherine, Freya, Dorothy, David, Julie, and Kathi.

Wherever our flaws, they will be ferreted out, and we, as individuals, will need to face them. We will probably find we have frightened ourselves into terrible anxiety for what, when seen in the light of unconditional love, isn't so bad or difficult to change after all.
— Elizabeth Earnest, therapist and High Wind board member, Windwatch, April 1987

The most important concept I took away from my experience with High Wind: finding ways to take important ideas out of their safe cocoons and pushing them into life.
— Milenko Matanovic, program leader, 2005 High Wind Survey

Katherine Collis leads international folk dance.

Saying goodbye at seminar's end is tough:
Katherine and Barbara.

Twentieth Anniversary Reunion group—returnees come from across the U.S., 1998.

Wrap-up sharing in the barn at the reunion.

> What influenced me most were the retreats with the Lorians. I was going through a very difficult time in my life, and the encouragement I found there to believe/trust my experiences with spirit gave me a foundation to build on slowly. I value very much those experiences and explorations at High Wind.
> — Susan Newstead, program participant, 2005 High Wind Survey

Bobby and Lynn leave for home (Chattanooga) on their Harley.

Last hug.

Reflections on the Appeal of High Wind and Similar Communities from High Wind Residents, Program Leaders, and Program Participants

High Wind stood as an especially attractive, inspiring model, for many values. An intentional community out in the country may or may not work, but a bona fide better way is always needed and needs to be demonstrated. Bel and Lisa are so forceful and practical in their idealism, I thought nearly anything could be accomplished.

— *Robert Thompson, program participant, 2005 High Wind Survey*

What's important is that High Wind exists and has created numerous opportunities for people to gain insight and to grow. "Master the possibilities" versus "Admiring the problems". . . . High Wind creates the opportunity to explore a vision of a healthy, whole world—one that meets the needs of this generation without jeopardizing needs of future generations (or minimally).

— *Tom McGinnity, program leader, 2005 High Wind Survey*

High Wind is a place of openness into which energy can flow unobstructed. I've sensed this energy as the always-present power and benevolence of the Universe being allowed to enter here. I can feel the consciousness of this universal energy deeply. A space has been cleared at High Wind for this consciousness to live. . . . High Wind is blessed because it has opened to the gifts of the Universe. And the gifts received by High Wind are reflected in the gifts it gives, gifts of love and warmth and support. Gifts of laughter and work and healing flourish here so that, in some way, each day feels like a day of birth, a day of renewal.

— *Jane Nauschultz, resident, Windwatch, June 1985*

Initiatives of the ilk of High Wind are sweet oases of twinkling light in the mired-up universe we live in. Initiatives of this sort are part of the thousand-points-of-light network. Anything positive. Anything contributing some light and positive energy to the planet. Anything serving to educate and bring connection to the life force is sacred.

— *Beth Herbert, program participant, 2005 High Wind Survey*

Community Celebrations and Rituals

Community is exhausting work on many levels. There is one facet, however, that periodically pulls us away from our mundane, daily tasks to lift our spirits and remind us of the overarching, grand world vision that brought us here, that keeps us steady.

We usher in the new seasons, perhaps with balloons and song. We create celebrations to mark significant events in our collective life, or to cheer a major accomplishment. At one point, we designate the little igloo dome in the hollow as our sanctuary and gather to sit in silence on jewel-toned cushions surrounding a bowl of field flowers; a standing flag outside signifies that meditation is in session. Sunday mornings those interested may gather to ponder whatever deeper topics come up; for a while, we argued points in *A Course in Miracles*. The pursuit of cosmic matters depends greatly on who's living in the community at any one time.

We've had waves of guys so fiercely concentrated on construction deadlines that the rest of us felt consumed by an overhanging macho energy. Then several strong "spiritual types" will join the community who draw us away into the woods and meadows to listen to the voices of nature that speak to us from a place of universal connection. Sometimes the instigators of rituals and games rise from our own ranks and sometimes they come from outside—as Native Americans who teach us Indian drumming and chanting, or about pipe ceremonies. Or at the Equinox sunrise, seminar participants may erect a cornstalk altar where they offer water to the earth mother. Or we'll gather at the sacred fire circle to perform an Indian balance dance. . . .

Indian balance dance: blessing the six directions at the sacred fire circle at sunrise, 1987. (Photograph courtesy of Dave Somsky.)

106

Cornstalk altar where Three-Community Seminar participant offers water to the earth at sunrise, 1984.

The land that had come to us on which to create this experiment was beginning to speak to us. The awareness and connection we felt with a strong guiding power, the sense of purpose, was poured into this patch of land. The meditations of individuals, the silent gatherings in the sanctuary domes, the seasonal celebrations and rituals we held, the philosophical conversations we delighted in—all seemed to seep into the ground we walked and worked and planted. Visitors who came to High Wind felt the land giving back this tranquility. The meadows and woods were healing and supporting; they lifted and renewed the spirits of the many who came.
 — Lisa Paulson, at a High Wind board retreat, "The High Wind Myth," 1996

In predawn darkness, everyone gathering slowly from the corners of the property, playing simple instruments. Mysterious flute sounds from the west meadow, an answer from the forest. Standing at the sacred circle to watch the red sun appear. More vigorous music now, spontaneous dancing around the flames. A tall altar of cornstalks and wind chimes silhouetted against the eastern sky. Ceremony and song . . . tears.
 — Lisa Paulson, describing a fall equinox celebration created by the Three-Community Seminar, Windwatch, October 1984

Spring equinox 1982: residents and friends gather on the future bioshelter site (the place of new beginnings) to send up balloons filled with ticker tape where each of us writes our dreams, after burning and burying thoughts of what we want to leave in the past.

Holiday gathering of community and friends in the farmhouse, 1983. *Front row:* Tiffany Smithson (holding unidentified baby), Cindy Smithson, Beth Herbert, Joann Martens, Priscilla Dean, Jim Priest, Marcia Kjos, and Lorri Rhyner; *back row:* Betsy Abert, Lisa and Bel Paulson, Lisa Smithson, and Leann Kjos.

Spiral dance at David and Louise's wedding, 1989.

Residents and visitors discuss *A Course in Miracles*. Terry Molner and Gordon Davidson (from Sirius) are on the left, 1984.

Harvest festival for neighbors and friends: games, music, High Wind products for sale, 1984.

The Sunday morning group meets in the bioshelter greenhouse to explore spiritual/philosophical questions, 1990.

An ex-resident of High Wind one time said that all community members were indeed very spiritual, but the group had no spiritual core. I wonder if this is true now. Can we see beyond our personal and sometimes complex belief systems to a deeper, more profound connection? Can we applaud each other's uniqueness, complete with all the baggage? . . . The bonds that keep us living and sharing at High Wind seem to go beyond the theories, practices and tools we use to experience spirituality in our lives.

— Marcia Kjos, resident, reflecting at a Sunday morning meeting, Windwatch, *Spring/Summer 1990*

Public Interface and Networking

Public interface, networking, and outreach have been a vital part of our agenda from the beginning. They are the backbone of our stated purpose of openness, of world service through demonstration and dialogue. People are curious about all aspects of our work and life; they want to see and learn about our technical innovations, our solar buildings, and organic farm. They're anxious for a glimpse inside this mysterious phenomenon—an experiment in simple communal living. Are the sustainable practices we subscribe to replicable in the wider society?

Tour group inspects the two small domes being built for low cost and maximum efficiency.

Visitors from France come to High Wind and also check out our bookstore in Milwaukee, 1989.

David leads tours to demonstrate energy-efficient applications; here he explains the solar panel he constructed on the chicken coop where he lives, 1984.

Visitors admire Jim's solar shower, which provides up to eight hot showers on a sunny day, 1987.

Geoff Kozeny (videographer for the Fellowship for Intentional Community) visits High Wind while networking among communities across the U.S., 1991. (Geoff died in October 2007 while completing a comprehensive DVD series showcasing life in many American communities.)

Milwaukee Public Television Channels 10/36 films a news segment about High Wind, 1983.

Ripples Do Go Out

Veterans of our offbeat educational offerings have gone on to express in many ways the visions they helped to create with us: started a natural foods restaurant; built low-energy homes; worked nationally and locally for peace; founded spiritual networks; planted organic gardens; went into alternative modes of teaching; entered the political arena with more universal, non-adversarial values; created worker-owned businesses; and on and on. . . .

An Israeli couple visited Findhorn some years ago and was inspired to go home and start an institute that works for deep-level communication, conciliation, and harmony between Arabs and Jews in Israel, one of the few efforts of its kind. Along the way, the couple joined High Wind, and last year, Ben visited us to brainstorm ways we might work closely in lessening world tensions.

A Milwaukee husband and wife who had participated in our classes since 1978 have set up a direct communication link with scientist friends they met in the former Soviet Union, and they are discretely exchanging books, ideas, and goodwill.

The twelve students who completed the 1984 Living/Learning Seminar in Three Communities reported that the experience had a more profound impact than all their years in universities—some say in all their life. One, a former New York taxi driver, is now working at a shelter for street people. One is in Norway at a biodynamic farm. Two are interning at High Wind.

— *Lisa Paulson*, Windwatch, *1986*

Ben and Bracha Yanoov traveled from Israel to participate in High Wind activities and give a workshop on communication skills, 1985.

Storyteller Elizabeth Matson chronicled the "Journey of the 12" for her Three-Community Seminar in 1989.

High Wind is the dearest place in the world to me. The impact in practical terms in my daily life seems so small: I go out of my way to ride the bus, I choose jobs I can get to by public transportation, I have a rain barrel and an electric (and a hand-powered) mower, I garden organically, I don't flush the toilet every single time, I practice yoga and T'ai Chi, and occasionally I still run. It's so little. And yet High Wind looms so large in my consciousness, in my sense of who I am and what I ought to be doing, how I should be living my life.
— Elizabeth Matson, program participant, 2005 High Wind Survey

Peter Seely shows volunteers how to braid garlic at Springdale Farm, the CSA (Community Supported Agriculture) he and his wife Bernadette created when they bought the land from High Wind.

High Wind connected with local, national, and international networks around a refreshing consciousness needed within individuals and organizations for a better world in the future. The trips to Findhorn and other intentional communities that Lisa, Bel, and David took during the formative years of High Wind inspired seminars, salons, workshops, summits, retreats, and tours whose content and processes engaged individuals and groups to be honest about current conditions and hopeful about the future.
— Bob Pavlik, program leader, 2005 High Wind Survey

Reflections on the Personal Impact of High Wind from Residents, Program Leaders, and Program Participants

The most important value I've taken away from my experience at High Wind: to be truly sustainable, I've got to make sure I put on my own oxygen mask before I help the others in the plane put theirs on. At the same time, I must remember that we truly are ONE and interdependent and responsible to and for one another.
— *Joy Decker, resident, 2005 High Wind Survey*

High Wind was key in opening me up to a conscious spiritual path, and I continue to explore this aspect of my life. Because of High Wind, my degree at UW-Milwaukee was in peace studies and I've continued on in the healing arts. . . . I'm still in touch with Elizabeth Matson from my Three-Community Seminar in 1984.
— *Kesha Engel, program participant, 2005 High Wind Survey*

I came to High Wind with no expectations—except for myself. I expected to encounter hard spiritual labor, and I have not been disappointed. Since moving here, I've been initiated into a mystery and have traveled into the labyrinth of myself. It's been difficult and frightening—I can only say I'm so glad it has happened here where I'm surrounded by people who care, who know what this kind of journey is about, and who are not frightened by or impatient with its process. As for the journey itself, there is much joy as well as fear. And it has been a spiral path, going in and out again. Energy and wisdom have grown in me, and I go on with a light heart.
— *Jan Christensen, shortly after arriving*
   to live in the community, Windwatch, January 1988,

My associations at High Wind helped me bring more purpose and questions to my practice as a Catholic. David Spangler's workshops, the accounts of High Wind board members on their spiritual journeys, and my interactions with board members helped me realize that my previous practice as a Catholic was way too narrow, biased, and unfulfilling and, equally as important, that I must grow in new ways in my spiritual journey.
— *Bob Pavlik, program leader, 2005 High Wind Survey*

Being an extremely private person, especially with my spiritual life, it's taken me many years to find a relationship with the magical workings of spirit that feel authentic to me. I needed to work much more one-to-one than in a group. Perhaps High Wind set me to delving into this.
— *Bethe Hagens, program leader, 2005 High Wind Survey*

I think through my connecting to High Wind and the community there that I am a better person for this. . . . It has altered my views on the job of education—education is broader than just teaching children. . . . I gained optimism from High Wind: I knew there was a better way, that a closer community is possible.
— *Susan Safran, program participant, 2005 High Wind Survey*

I speak up for sustainable, conscious development whenever I have the voice to make a difference. I promote and use Fair Trade products as I'm educated to; it makes a difference, and I'm willing to keep growing and understanding how together we can create a better world.
— *Kesha Engel, program participant, 2005 High Wind Survey*

High Wind truly helped me to find my path in my life, and I will always be grateful.
— *Barbara Prendergast (junior), program participant, 2005 High Wind Survey*

Chapter Six

The New Stewards

Community and collaboration are a challenging and always changing set of relationships. Staying current with the needs of a collective, including nature as a partner, is a real dance, an act of continual rebalancing. We are only beginning to get clear on the steps that work for this turn of the spiral.

— Freya Secrest, Lorian program leader, 2005 High Wind Survey

At High Wind there was a strong sense of shared purpose, yet at the same time there was recognition of the value of personal identity, of uniqueness. Unlike a number of strictly egalitarian communities with income-sharing and greater interdependency, we always considered ourselves a bunch of "feisty individuals." We encouraged tolerance of differences, and when intuitive decisions and actions deviated from projected group plans, we listened and tried to honor them.

Because we'd been listed in the directories of major communities around the world and had gotten much publicity, we were receiving more and more inquiries and visitors. It became difficult for the residents to handle such volume—feeding, housing, and interacting with those who wrote, called, or just showed up on our doorstep. There were also folks who came, their eyes gleaming with visions of "utopia," who were disgruntled when they found our earlier pattern of close-knit living and working together—with communal cooking and meals and all such expected "groupiness"—had gradually been

replaced by more private lifestyles. By the late 1980s, there were more families, and several had built their own solar homes. People were feeling the need for greater autonomy, a chance to explore their own creative projects and professions without the community breathing down their necks. They were tired of the obligatory meetings and conscripted duties.

LETTING GO OF OUR IMAGE

Eventually, some twelve years down the road, the last wave of residents began to burn out. This was partly because High Wind never generated enough money to pay its people, and either their small savings had run out or they had to scramble for outside jobs. People also just became worn down by the constant responsibility for the program logistics and taking care of increasing numbers of guests. They began, as well, to feel frustrated at spending too many hours in meetings. For these reasons, after a couple of years of serious debate in early 1992, we made the momentous decision to let go of our image and to make it known publicly that we were no longer an intentional community.

We had seen that the initial burst of energy people had brought, an eagerness to give over everything "to serve the greater whole," was giving way to a new recognition: it was wiser to avoid burnout by balancing the needs of High Wind with taking care of personal well-being, nourishing couple and family relationships, and concentrating on earning a real living. These changing agendas prompted us to decide to separate the community into two parts.

SHIFTS IN COMMUNITY STRUCTURE

The High Wind Learning Center (our major focus after the bioshelter was more or less completed) was oriented to public outreach. Even after the dissolution of the intentional community, it continued to honor the educational mandate of our non-profit status by operating guest and seminar programs, and was involved in a worldwide network of activities. It was run by a small group who were fired up by this particular mission; it was to be a business rather like the other on-site private cottage industries. For a short time, we hired a full-time manager, paying an almost "normal" salary. This seemed to make good sense; anyone putting in time needed to cover their living expenses. However, we found it also opened the door to a range of problems common in the "real world" that had been mostly absent during the earlier years at High Wind.

> In order to carry on our present programs, we've had to "borrow" a lot: borrow against our psychic security and personal financial well-being. Doing that for very long can burn people out. We need a subtle but pervasive shift. We need to be centered and graceful in our hour-to-hour conduct, within ourselves and with each other, first and foremost. If we can do that, we will have something to give, which is why we're here in the first place.
> — David Lagerman, High Wind resident, *Windwatch*, April 1987

When money entered the picture, suddenly remuneration became the all-important issue. "What am I worth? What am I owed?" they asked, rather than "What's needed? How can I help?" We'd had an inkling of this shift when occasionally we paid one resident (a pittance) to cook for a large program. For the first time, other members began to see themselves as "grunts" not adequately appreciated or rewarded for their own stressful responsibilities. When we began hiring managers, one could say that, in effect, the vital, cohesive life of the community ended.

The other group on the land consisted of those who had built or bought energy-efficient houses at High Wind, deciding to put down more permanent roots. We could no longer afford to have volunteers living in our public buildings for free (the farmhouse, bioshelter, coop, and barn), so those folks were asked to leave. (By way of explanation, when we first let go of the intentional community aspect to become more of a retreat center, we needed the public buildings to house paying guests and to rent to outside groups.) At first, the group who owned homes called itself an "ecovillage." Some, though, thought this sounded too self-important, and so we opted to be simply a "neighborhood" of friends sharing the same ecological values and ideals of living in harmony with each other and with nature, but being free to pursue individual paths. The fellowship of having lived through intense past experiences together created a strong bond that will always hold.

Some of the High Wind land was (informally) set aside in conservancy to be stewarded, untouched, into the foreseeable future. Land owned by individuals was designated for homes and private businesses. The educational complex included the public buildings, which were to be used for seminars and for housing guests and Learning Center staff. Through this division, we aimed for the better of two worlds: one of independent living with an autonomy of finances (and souls), and the other, the educational group, cooperating on financial, programmatic, and administrative responsibilities as well as philosophical/ecological purposes. It came down to seeking a healthy balance between working for the greater good and being good neighbors while enjoying personal freedom, with residents free to move back and forth between these two modes.

It's interesting to note that now, after letting go of the intense, close-knit community structure, we've actually felt a *greater* closeness and caring for each other. We come together because we *want* to rather than because it's an obligation. An example: several years ago one of the residents not involved in the core programming became deathly ill, and spontaneously we gathered on our hill every evening for several weeks to meditate and visualize him getting well. Against all expectations, he pulled out of the coma, began to breathe on his own, came home, and

> I see High Wind as an avant-garde group that has been able to learn from its experiences and modify its course. As Kahlil Gibran said, "You shot your arrow in the air." Now you can fade away, like old soldiers, and throw your support to various environmental groups.
>
> — *Wil Kraegel, UWM professor, 2005 High Wind Survey*

credited our prayer circle with helping to save his life. This man and his wife felt connected to High Wind as they hadn't previously. (Bill died later as he did have severe heart problems—but he, his wife Rosalie, and we felt there had been a renewed energy and a burst of hope from the healing power of love and prayer.) Of course, part of the reason for the new tranquility could be more pedestrian: when the community dissolved, so did the conflicts and animosities.

IN RETROSPECT

Along the way, High Wind had gradually been acquiring more land. Early on, Bel and I donated the farmhouse, barn, and coop and some land around these buildings. Then, in 1982, a wealthy member bought sixty-two acres just east of us that High Wind was able to purchase in 1988. This included the additional set of farm buildings that became Springdale Farm—the CSA where Peter and Bernadette Seely began growing vegetables and fruits on twenty-five acres. Several years later, they bought this land from High Wind to run their very successful business privately, although they've tied in with us in many ways and have incorporated our tours and educational programs into their farm projects.

In the late 1980s, several High Wind Associates who had been donating money regularly to support the nonprofit (even though they didn't live here) stepped forward to buy twenty acres on the other side of High Wind that was in danger of being sold for a subdivision. By 1998, High Wind comprised 128 acres: some owned by the Association and dedicated to the educational/retreat work or kept wild in conservancy and some owned privately. We gained an additional buffer in 1996 when a board member bought twenty acres on the west boundary. Over a span of nearly thirty years, we had managed to save our valley from development.

Looking back at this period, more than a dozen years after the dissolution of the intentional community, we can note that since 1977, thousands of people have visited High Wind—and probably had their lives affected on practical and/or inspirational levels. Some seventy folks found a place to live, relatively inexpensively, for stretches of months or years, contributing their particular ideas, dreams, enthusiasms, energies, and financial resources.

THE SAGA CONTINUES: PLYMOUTH INSTITUTE IS BORN

Even though the structure of the community had scaled back dramatically, we found it wasn't quite time to turn in our union cards. The seemingly quite autonomous and contrary spirit of High Wind was cooking up some more work for us.

In 1992, another property came up for sale, across the road from Springdale Farm to our north. This was Silver Springs, a unique, 144-acre piece of land with nineteen artesian wells and innumerable springs that daily poured out over two-and-a-half million gallons of some of the purest water in the state to become the headwaters of the Onion River. There was a trout hatchery with raceways and twenty ponds, a conference center/ inn with a commercial restaurant and kitchen, and four large, luxury chalets for rent tucked into a lovely pine forest, with a high scenic ridge of hardwoods and meadowland at its back.

An intriguing historical detail is that in the early 1840s, Silver Springs was the site of one of this country's Utopian Socialist settlements, sparked by the ideas of Frenchman Charles Fourier. No doubt it was chosen because of its unique water resource, as was also the case for Native Americans centuries before. (Further information is provided in Appendix Two.)

Several people at High Wind got together hastily with colleagues from around Wisconsin and Illinois to make an offer to purchase the property, having only twenty-four hours to decide before it would be sold to developers. We felt this was a precious resource that *had* to be saved, and we were able to come up with the downpayment but had very little more for operating expenses. Our plan was that we would continue to rent the chalets, run the restaurant and the fish business, and possibly sell the water for bottling. Our expectation was that these enterprises would be able to sustain the property and finance the educational work and ecological experiments and demonstrations that were our real interests.

A core of talented people was brought in to help form two new corporations with two new boards. We created a for-profit company called Silver Springs of Plymouth and another nonprofit, Plymouth Institute, to be the umbrella for all the work, both at Silver Springs and High Wind.

Change Is in the Air

By the early 1990s, the stamina required to maintain the highest sense of purpose in our close-knit intentional community is flagging. The physical energy needed to handle the ever-more complicated logistics and keeping the facilities up to snuff is an increasing burden. All the mandated togetherness is getting us down, too.

And so we make the momentous, collective decision to let go of this image. We decide to become, instead, a more relaxed neighborhood of good friends who share the same values we've held together over the years. We would have the freedom to pursue individual interests and projects at our own pace.

Summer at High Wind: Bioshelter and wind chime.

Autumn landscape with three High Wind domes, bioshelter (upper left), and barn (upper right).

It was a verdant, languorous summer during which we at High Wind indulged in luminous conversations and posted dreamy scenarios on the ethereal web—an invisible connecting linkage in the ethers. Then, with the crisping of autumn, the clouds of pale yellow butterflies disappeared and suddenly we woke up to the sharp reality that a long, familiar chapter in our life and work was closing and a new one is being written.

— *Lisa Paulson, in a report on the short-lived Learning Community, created as an effort to rekindle the energy of the early intellectually and philosophically stimulating activities of High Wind, 1996*

Communities aren't end results, but are the laboratories of the world. . . . God is evident only when we goof; he teaches through our mistakes.

— *Milenko Matanovic, leader at Lorian-High Wind Seminar, "Applying the Vision and Principles in Community," July 1983*

Plymouth Institute Is Created, an Offshoot of High Wind

With our scaled back staff, we gradually shift our emphasis from running back-to-back educational events to renting the bioshelter and farmhouse to outside groups for their own retreats.

Then, in 1992, with a sudden burst of fresh momentum, to everyone's surprise, Plymouth Institute is created. Bel and I, with several gifted new friends, seize an opportunity to purchase the spectacular 144-acre Silver Springs trout farm just to our north. Our first priority is to rescue a property that is destined to be sold imminently as a subdivision. We also see fantastic opportunities with its myriad assets: a unique water resource, a conference center/restaurant, and rental chalets.

Plymouth Institute is gaining a reputation for avant garde ideas in the broader field of teaching. Consultations and educational "summits" draw key thinkers and innovators from across the country to our conference facility to brainstorm radical changes for our Wisconsin schools and colleges.

The newly created Plymouth Institute organizing group, 1992. *Top row, from left:* Kathy Kennard, Bil Becker, Lisa; *front:* Jim Kennard, Bethe Hagens, and Bel.

Microhydro workshop at Silver Springs, the base of Plymouth Institute, 1992.

Unforeseen Challenges

Over the next several years, we had difficulty making a success of our new businesses and gradually had to let them go. We dissolved the restaurant within six months, the fish operation never became profitable, and we couldn't get a contract for the water. We continued to rent out the chalets, but, overall, the property required considerably more money than we were taking in.

For two years we did receive a substantial boost that paid the bills. The Milwaukee Public Schools awarded Plymouth Institute a large contract to have seven hundred inner city middle school children come in small groups to experience staying on the land for periods of one to five days. We devised hands-on programs in aquaculture, organic farming, solar energy, and nature study. This was a natural, since over the years Bel had been involved in innovation and change within the Milwaukee school system, at one point helping to create the first *public* Waldorf School in the U.S. and later creating the Global Learning Center, an out-of-the-box experiment for middle schoolers. (The program was not located in a specific building, but rather classes were held in various strategic landmark locations around the city.) Both of these innovative programs involved mainly inner city kids.

> The Silver Springs property represented perhaps unrealistic business ideals, but ultimately the land at last seems to have found its way into good hands for the future. I sometimes had the feeling that our mission was visualized mostly in aesthetic terms—what would be beautiful, environmental, sustainable, communal—rather than political and realistic. I'm one to lead from the heart. I think all of us were, with a few significant exceptions. . . . And, ultimately, this got us in trouble
>
> — *Bethe Hagens, Plymouth Institute leader, 2005 High Wind Survey*

Our two new boards had people from influential spheres in Milwaukee and Chicago who brought expertise and fresh vision and support. There was a lot of energy around the idea of creating a consortium of colleges and universities and school systems. Participants would come to our facilities for special training and experiential learning, meetings, and retreats. A prominent new foundation was giving large grants for innovative kinds of construction and approached us for ideas.

Together with an imported architect and water expert, Plymouth Institute Board of Directors members Bethe Hagens and Bil Becker were instrumental in designing a spectacular, world-class eco-conference center. The design incorporated every sustainable technology imaginable, including micro-hydro power from the artesian wells to generate electricity and exotic touches such as a "SkyHoops Greenspace Dome" observatory, with waterfalls and hanging gardens, and even a funicular connecting terraced guest rooms cantilevered off a cliff face. The foundation was highly intrigued, but no funding resulted.

When it became clear we weren't going to make it economically on our existing businesses, we began to push an idea that had been close to our hearts from the beginning—the primary reason we were there, in fact—to create an ecological village on the ridge above Silver Springs. We named it SpringLedge. Following a very successful national ecovillage conference that we convened in 1995, there was real impetus to set the plan in motion, and a number of potential participants scrambled to buy in.

The ecovillage could become a demonstration for a new settlement—a stunning alternative to the rural sprawl now popping up all over the area and threatening delicate ecosystems. It would showcase a "constructed wetlands" (for biological sewage treatment), hybrid energy production with both wind and sun, "green" buildings, and clustered housing that would leave large areas of commonly owned wild space. We envisioned about twenty-one half-acre sites. Our plan could be a model to stem the tide of chaotic construction by the hordes fleeing tension-laden, unsafe cities. Spring-Ledge could easily pay off the land, we figured, relieve us of a crippling mortgage, and bring in a whole new tier of people to support our educational work.

Local newspaper cartoon after the ecovillage proposal was rejected.

A Lesson in Diplomacy

Unfortunately, the project didn't work out. Neighbors in our conservative township were suspicious of our "radical" concepts, and they even publicly branded us

"communists" for advocating clustered housing and owning land in common. They brought in lawyers and packed the town meetings with very vocal objections—the upshot being that the town board imposed a blanket moratorium, making it impossible to implement a project such as ours. We considered other alternatives, but because we couldn't carry on with the stiff payments to keep Silver Springs, we were forced to place it on the market.

We began to search for the "right" buyer who would be sympathetic to our concerns, would help us preserve the entire valley (High Wind and Silver Springs) as an intact ecosystem, and with whom we might have an interactive, cooperative working relationship. For two years, we held out, Bel and I personally shouldering the mortgage to fend off developers who were greedily licking their chops. Happily, a wealthy regional businessman came to the rescue, buying the property in 1999 and then turning over most of the 144 acres of land to the State Department of Natural Resources. The man-made ponds and waterways were returned to their pristine, natural state. The restaurant/conference space was not turned over to the Department of Natural Resources, but rather was sold to an individual.

In hindsight, we realized our mistake: we were so enamored and engrossed with mapping out our grand innovative plan that we neglected the necessary political spadework with our conservative neighbors, to explain thoroughly to them the potential benefits for the town and region. The informational meetings we organized at the town hall after the fat was already in the fire were too late to change peoples' minds.

One very positive side effect, though, was the enormous amount of press coverage as the whole case unfolded. The local Plymouth and Sheboygan papers were fascinated and pretty uniformly supportive of our plan; week after week, admiring statements took over the headlines and editorial pages. If we were out to educate the public about impending environmental dangers and the beauty of sustainable technologies, we couldn't have found a more effective forum.

Picking Up the Pieces: A Fresh Look at High Wind

With both the newer corporations dissolved (Plymouth Institute and Silver Springs of Plymouth), the focus turned once again to High Wind. Our tired flagship had been subsumed in the splash and glamour of all the new people and technical/entrepreneurial energy rushing to center stage, but now High Wind seemed to represent the clarity and simplicity of a lost, even nostalgic, era.

For over twenty years, High Wind had held in its sacred lands and in the hearts of all those drawn to its original vision, a power that still demanded recognition and preservation. We felt we were being called on to slow down and listen to where we might next be led.

A number of brief initiatives flamed up over the next couple of years. With a short-term grant from a Chicago foundation, we hired several full-time managers to oversee maintenance and rental of our public facilities for the High Wind Retreat Center. Then some old and new devotees (always hungering for that ever-alluring sense of community and common purpose) rallied to envision a "High Wind Learning Community." A closely bonded group of intellectuals and idealists would form to talk about the implications of "higher consciousness" and to work at projecting a more mature wisdom into the existing culture—as well as infusing High Wind itself with new life and goals.

We also hung on to the elegant concept of the ecovillage as an answer to chaotic development; after the town's moratorium was lifted, eleven acres of High Wind's west fields were surveyed into five building sites, and this time the town approved the project. Compared to SpringLedge, this "Thistledown" settlement would be very scaled down but could still demonstrate a biological sewage treatment system and other sustainable features. Again buyers lined up almost immediately.

> Because High Wind dedicated itself to new ideas, it had a natural and expected tension with the mainstream society. Out of this tension came limitations of support, funding, and so on. Limitations came with the territory.
>
> — *Milenko Matanovic, Lorian leader, 2005 High Wind Survey*

SpringLedge—A Lost Opportunity

With the acquisition of the Silver Springs property with its rich natural resources, visions of multiple, sustainable inventions and demonstrations proliferate at a great rate. These efforts culminate in an on-site sophisticated blueprint for a state-of-the-art ecological village that we would call SpringLedge.

Although lauded by national experts, our vision for an ecovillage is ahead of its time, and our rural neighbors vote it down. In a packed town meeting, people jump up to attack our plan for clustered housing, shared wells, a biological waste treatment system, and commonly held greenspace. "You're communists!" they shout. "Why don't you move to Russia?" (!)

Walking the pine forest to dedicate the Silver Springs property, 1992.

Lisa and Bil Becker with John Hinde (expert consultant on water culture and purification), 1992.

Full Stop?

Then, in the midst of this flurry to reactivate High Wind, all of us living on site, as well as the ever-vigilant, principled High Wind Board of Directors, sat back on our heels, took a deep breath, and began to question where we were heading. It became increasingly clear we were tired of repairing our aging buildings, and for what? We were about *education*, not merely renting out facilities to outsiders. Also, several years back we had promised ourselves to keep certain designated parts of our land in wilderness, and Thistledown (even if ecologically sound) would involve development of our peaceful west fields. After a summer of exciting brainstorming sessions, the Learning Community energy petered out, and we also vetoed going ahead with Thistledown.

Now came a really radical decision. Having lost our interest in continuing to maintain buildings and pay taxes but still intent on stewarding open land that nourished our souls, our board decided to sell the public campus of High Wind: the farmhouse, barn, coop, bioshelter, and dome home, with small amounts of land around them. In this case, it would be absolutely critical to find a buyer or buyers in tune with everything our credo had stood for and not let down the thousands who had followed our progress and cheered our efforts for so many years.

After quickly passing the fateful, unanimous vote, all of us on the board looked at each other in astonishment. Evidently it *was* time, and we could

> I wish High Wind had been sustainable as a community; I wish I could have become a resident. But it remains, always, a powerful touchstone in my life.
> — *Elizabeth Matson, High Wind program participant , 2005 High Wind Survey*

all see it. I think others were surprised that Bel and I (especially I—High Wind was my *child!*) could let it all go so easily. But we recognized we had done what we had set out to accomplish. A great many lives had been touched, we'd created a concrete demonstration of community and sustainability, and we'd initiated some important, widespread dialogue about how people might better relate to each other, to nature, and to spirit.

ENTER THE BUDDHISTS

Again, the overlighting angel of High Wind (or so we liked to imagine) sprang into action, and before very long, we had our buyers. Actually, two groups responded, both Buddhist. Richard Zenyo Brandon, from a Japanese Zen style in Chicago, had been bringing his meditation students here for years. In 2001, he purchased the lower complex of buildings including the farmhouse, barn, and coop plus the requisite three acres of land. He called his new center Bright Dawn.

Alan Anderson and his wife, Sue Firer, bought the bioshelter in 2002. They had been bringing retreat groups to High Wind for a long time. (In fact, Alan had taken one of Bel's futures classes in the early 1990s). For years, he and Sue had shepherded the (Tibetan Buddhist) Shambhala Center of Milwaukee and had, as well, been active in two larger Shambhala centers in Colorado and Vermont.

Not long afterwards, Alan and Sue began to dream and talked to us about creating a substantial Midwest Shambhala Retreat Center to serve the entire midsection of the country. One goal: to become a pilot among other new Shambhala meditation "land" centers by emphasizing sustainability, land stewardship, peace, "authentic leadership," and social action. This could be a beautiful segue to our focus at High Wind. In early 2007, they acquired thirty-three additional acres of land that Bel and I owned personally (most of it we donated). The world leader of Shambhala, Sakyong Mipham Rimpoche ("Rimpoche" means teacher), duly blessed the property in a colorful, smoky ceremony.

After two years of deliberation, the Sakyong gave the center its new identity: Windhorse. Diana Mukpo, in her book *Dragon Thunder: My Life with Chogyam Trungpa,* describes the Tibetan concept of Windhorse as bringing the powerful, clean energy of the wind down to earth to be harnessed and ridden purposefully, as one would ride a horse. This is the energy that arises when we create the conditions for stability and happiness.

HIGH WIND FOUNDATION NOW FUNDS OTHERS

With cash from the property sales suddenly swelling our bank account, the High Wind board for the first time enjoyed the astonishing luxury of not holding out its hand for support. Immediately, with the help of our wonderful, long-time, local pro bono attorney, Mel Blanke, we took steps to grow the principal and to create a foundation that could begin to *give money away.*

What a novelty! Within the first year, we had students from an inner city school experiencing a nature camp and helped save a venerable summer kids' camp in danger of folding. When a Milwaukee parish in a low-income area came to us in 2006 for advice on making their church buildings more energy efficient, our sizable donation served as an incentive to get the work done and to serve as an urban model.

Other new projects are currently underway. We're galvanizing the Interfaith Council of Milwaukee to consider joint sustainability goals. We're helping fund a nature program for inner city schools through Milwaukee's Urban Ecology Center. A loan to Milwaukee's first Fair Trade store is helping to buy inventory directly from craftspeople in low-income countries, enabling them to work from their homes. A plan Bel had floated years earlier, to create a Sustainable Futures Institute that could include serious educational tie-ins with universities and a think tank to design new sustainability curricula, has crept into the conversation again. Some board members are considering lead roles. On several fronts, there are people picking up where we left off—with new forms that embody the values of High Wind's past work.

As for those of us former communitarians still living on the land, our stint with the annual national solar homes tour still takes place each fall, and people continue to call for technical consults. Others, thinking about starting or joining a community, call or write or visit to pick our brains about our experience. We host tours and talks for groups, often educators. To keep in touch, I send out infrequent updates to friends and supporters who have followed our journey over the years.

This brings the saga of High Wind up to date. The history stands firm, the mantle is now shared, and the twenty residents—including community veterans, several more recent homeowners, and the Buddhist newcomers—are coexisting gracefully, sharing occasional potlucks, books, DVDs, walks in the woods, good conversation, in-house concerts, and more. We watch out for each other as we also happily "do our own thing." All of us are held in the loving embrace of our enchanted, healing land: the carpet of white trillium under the oaks and maples in May, the fiery golds and crimsons of autumn, waist-high grasses and wildflowers in the summer meadows, the quiet black and white forest of winter. . . .

And then there is the WIND—so often the wind: the freight train roar that begins in the deep glacial kettles at the bottom of our woods, accelerating until it bursts from the trees. Updrafts that toss billowy thunderheads across an August sky and give the circling redtails a free glide. Gale forces from the east that send February blizzards howling across the spine of our high, open ridge so fiercely that we can barely stand up. And then a gentle sighing among the towering pines on the path to the hermitage.

Wind is the signature energy that has carried those stewarding these High Wind lands for the past quarter century. Now its new custodians are charged to ride it into the future.

Always the Wind.

Inner City Kids' Programs at Plymouth Institute

A grant from the Milwaukee Public Schools brings seven hundred inner city middle schoolers to Plymouth Institute over a three-year period. They are exposed to solar energy, aquaculture, organic agriculture, and nature. Typically they come for three days and two nights, sleeping in the High Wind barn and eating at the farmhouse. One very successful segment involves teaching survival skills in our woods by members of the Wisconsin Air National Guard. Colonel Bob Schick insists on sleeping in a tent along with the kids and takes them into the meadow after dark to hunt each other with night vision goggles. The program culminates with a surprise visit from the regional general. Instructors and students (with flags they've designed and made themselves) stand at attention as the giant Blackhawk helicopter lands in our field.

Kids on Peter's tractor at Springdale Farm, 1993.

Catching a ride at the farm, 1993.

Lunch at the farmhouse, 1993.

Learning to build fires in the rain with Air National Guard reservists, 1995.

This past year was total involvement with the Milwaukee Public School System. The idea was that this could begin to prepare students for twenty-first century vocations. They had a great time, and some parts were highly successful. We included a challenge course that necessitated cooperation (low ropes, etc.). Then the final two weeks we had a chance to bring in the Air National Guard (!) to run a survival training. They designed a compass course in our woods, and the kids found their way to various stations where they could practice skills they learned: first aid, starting fires in the rain, Morse code signals, purifying water, cooking in the wild. There was a lot of fancy technological equipment brought in that kids could use (e.g. night vision goggles). Some of us had been reluctant to import the military, as it seemed the antithesis of all we stand for. Yet after spending ten hours and more with the groups in the field, I did an about-face, realizing I'd formed some rather black-and-white opinions. We found the guardsmen (and women) very gentle, human, and superbly equipped to share knowledge in an exciting way. The kids loved it. The guardsmen were good precisely because they weren't invested in making kids learn. They had information that could be taken or not, and it was shared in a low-key, humorous way. (Of course, it helped to have a very high ratio of instructors to children.)

— Lisa Paulson, from a letter to Sue Brooks, 1995

Lori Saillé shares nature lore, 1993.

Kids inspect seedlings in Springdale greenhouse, 1995.

David demonstrates how to create fire with the sun and mirrors.

Moving dirt at Springdale, 1993.

Reservist instructors and our kids welcome the commanding general landing in our west meadow, 1995.

Back to Findhorn to Speak at a Conference

In 1998, Bel and I are back in Scotland where the High Wind dream was originally conceived. We're asked to speak at Findhorn's annual fall conference, this year focused on "Ecovillages and Sustainable Communities." The cautionary tale of our own thwarted ecovillage experiment is recounted.

We find at Findhorn itself an even stronger push now for hands-on demonstrations of living lightly and mindfully on the earth. Stunning examples of innovative technologies and practices that significantly shrink their carbon footprint abound. Gathered for the conference are scores of leaders and members of intentional communities from many countries, and we find it especially comforting to swap stories and discover that our challenges at High Wind are universal—"founders' dilemmas."

"Living Machine" handles Findhorn's sewage by cycling it through water tanks containing plants, bacteria, and other living organisms—the idea pioneered for the New Alchemy Institute's bioshelters, 1998.

Michael Shaw explains the concept of the "Living Machine" that he built for the community, 1998.

Bag End, Findhorn's experimental ecovillage, perhaps the best example in Britain of sustainable design and use of materials, 1998.

True conservation: residents create private living spaces in the community with recycled Scotch whiskey barrels, 1998.

The nature sanctuary at Findhorn is used for meditation and a capella singing, 1998.

Conference attendees gather for meals at the Community Center, 1998.

The lunch buffet includes artfully displayed salads often decorated with flowers from the gardens, 1998.

High Wind Sells Its Public Buildings to Two Buddhist Groups

By 2001, High Wind has wound down most of its public programs on the land, and its residents (now only those who own their own homes) and the board of directors are ready to refocus their energy. Some of us are prepared to help more groups in mainstream society to understand the magnitude of the new cultural imperative and to implement elements of sustainability on practical levels.

We also realize that we're ready to let go of our public buildings, a radical move that will truly set us free from the all-consuming responsibilities of the past dozen years. Happily, we find two groups that relate closely to many of our core values. They love and revere the land as we do, and they are focusing on awareness of the deeper dimension of life—as we have attempted to do.

In 2001, Richard Zenyo Brandon brings his years of Japanese-oriented Buddhist meditation leadership experience in Chicago to High Wind when he purchases the farmhouse/barn/coop complex.

Bright Dawn Buddhists

Richard Zenyo Brandon, ("Meditating Sun"), founder of Bright Dawn Home Spread.

Building on the Zen style and practices established by the Reverend Gyomay Kubose, Richard leads spiritual awareness treks for retreatants on the land and weaves work projects and simple living into quiet times of reflection and ritual. After his arrival at High Wind, he is inducted as a "lay minister" by the Kbose Dharma Legacy, doing business as Bright Dawn Institute.

Early in 2002, Alan Anderson and Sue Firer, teachers of Tibetan Shambhala Buddhism in Milwaukee, buy the bioshelter for a rural meditation/retreat center. Like Richard, their deep commitments and values parallel much of what High Wind has anchored firmly over the past thirty years. Then, in 2007, a combination of sale and donation brings an additional thirty-three acres west of the farmhouse into the Shambhala orbit. Sakyong Mipham, world head of Shambhala Buddhism, names this center Windhorse.

The new stewards have arrived!.

Reverend Koyo Kubose conducts Richard Brandon's ordination as a lay minister with the symbolic "shaving the head" ceremony.

A Bright Dawn retreat group meditates at High Wind's sacred fire circle.

Shambhala Buddhists

Sakyong Mipham, world head of Shambhala Buddhism, visits Windhorse. Seated in the bioshelter shrine room, *left to right:* Alan Anderson, Sakyong Mipham, and Sue Firer.

Buddhist banners and prayer flags herald the new ownership of the bioshelter.

The Sakyong comes to bless and dedicate the new Shambhala land in a smoky ceremony.

Would I Live in Community Again?

Initiatives like High Wind are beacons of inspiration for peaceful, cooperative living with each other and the planet. Even through the really tough times and decisions, the willingness to engage is significant.

— *Joann Martens, High Wind resident, 2005 High Wind Survey*

*I*n August 2005, the High Wind Board of Directors sent a questionnaire to people, nationwide, who had either lived in our intentional community (roughly 1981 to 1992) or had been involved in related activities over the twenty-five-year span of our community's ongoing work. (The 2005 High Wind Survey was designed and the data analyzed by Robert Pavlik, Marquette University professor and High Wind board member.) We were curious to find out what the impact might have been on the thinking and lives of people touched by our ideas as we spun them out as dreams and projects. We sent the survey to 180 of those who had maintained the closest contact with High Wind.

It was interesting to note that the most upbeat and unfailingly positive replies to our questionnaire did not come from those who had lived in the community but rather came from people who had participated in High Wind-related events as well as served on our various boards. In contrast, the communitarians shared that they often found their financial security next to zero, the flexibility and skills required constantly stretched,

and the ability to adjust to sharing lives closely with a group of heterogeneous strangers held up to scrutiny—not to mention the stamina needed to sit through endless group meetings for every decision. Yet one key former community resident concluded that despite the ups and downs (or maybe because of them), in the end the experience was a "perfect" learning mechanism.

The final survey question for those who had lived at High Wind was: "Would you live in a community again?" Bel and I wrote our answers separately without showing them to each other. Here's how we answered the question.

Lisa

No, I wouldn't choose to live in community again. Frankly, I wouldn't have the stamina to do it all again. And after so much intensity, when we seemed to almost live in each other's heads, it was wonderful to just take a rest from all that. I realized how much I prized my freedom, my privacy, and the solitude I could indulge in when I needed it. It felt as though I had paid my dues, done my bit to inch public awareness along.

It was an incredible experience—from its buildup and preparation from 1976 to 1981 and then through some twelve more years of intense togetherness. We were a very earnest, idealistic little group committed to living the experiment, to attempt modeling a more honest, more conscious, "clean" way of living than we felt we were seeing in the world at large.

At various times, there was both exhilaration and terrible pain, successes and gratifying public recognition, as well as personal and collective dark periods with false starts and stumbles. There was often an excruciating flashlight shone on each of our foibles and missteps—and then the wonderful, close friendships and just plain fun as we labored shoulder to shoulder and knew we were breaking new ground in this corner of Sheboygan County. There was personal growth and greater self-understanding. There was validation of what we were about, even though at times it seemed we'd crawl forward a step and then fall back two steps. Often it was hard to see what we were accomplishing, what we were achieving, and what we stood for in the eyes of the public; we were too close to it and tended to judge ourselves mercilessly.

So it was quite wonderful and even amazing to look back and realize that I had stuck it out and could feel positive about the whole experience. I knew it had been valuable, important. I think most of the others in the community felt the same.

But when we decided to loosen the bonds we were holding ourselves in—the lock-step closeness in how we functioned together, made decisions, and assessed our interpersonal relationship

skills obsessively in regular meetings—it felt not only right but enabled us to draw a huge collective sigh of relief. We could say "We did it!" and not feel guilty about morphing into a more loosely supportive neighborhood of friends, suddenly free to pursue our own passions and interests. It needn't mean giving up the values we'd championed so fiercely about conservation and a sustainable lifestyle. We realized we might even become more effective in our loosely structured setting as neighbors with shared values when we weren't under constant group scrutiny. We could also flower as individuals.

I can't exactly say what I'd do differently if I were to do it again. As some have noted, with all the stumbling toward creating something good and worthwhile, in the end it was really "perfect." The joys, the pain. It was a glorious way to learn and to point others on a path of awareness too. But I wouldn't want to try it again—not for myself anyway.

Perhaps a better model would be a less rigidly structured regime with more viability or longevity. The Israeli kibbutzniks after a while often opted out of their strictly communal situations to join or create the moshavim (where families had their own homes and people could hold paying jobs, but where there was still a strong community cohesion). Maybe a similar structure could work better here. Maybe the answer is some kind of cohousing community. But we all often remark that we wouldn't be the close group still living at High Wind if we hadn't gone through the "bath of fire" together. We'd be just a bunch of exurbanites living in energy efficient houses in the same vicinity. We had shared a lot, and that is a precious bond.

Now the High Wind board has a chance to strike out in new directions, to carry the lessons learned over the past twenty-five years to a new generation that increasingly is realizing that the very survival of our society and our Earth are in jeopardy. I can certainly muster enthusiasm for such an initiative.

Lisa's response, with slight modifications, is reprinted with permission from the Fall 2006 issue of Communities *magazine.*

Bel

The commitment to live in an alternative or intentional community such as a Findhorn or High Wind is, in essence, to grapple in a very concrete way with the search for a new vision of society. It's committing to a vision of sustainable living in your daily life (e.g. the shelter you construct and live in, the food you produce and eat, the transportation you use, the institutions you support regarding such matters as governance, and how money is earned and spent). It requires patterns of human relationships that favor cooperation over competition, sharing resources in contrast to seeking all you can for yourself, listening to people whose ideas you don't accept, and making decisions based on consensus instead of voting (majority/minority). As this paradigm is fleshed out from rhetoric to actual living, it comes face

High Wind's influence on my life and work? I now teach college courses in sustainable futures and sustainable design, and I infuse my work with globalism and justice.... High Wind was my first real exposure to another "society" and way of thinking.

— *Pamm Steffen, High Wind program participant , 2005 High Wind Survey*

to face with the prevailing mainstream culture—which is not sustainable, is organized around political/social/economic hierarchy, and is driven by short-run goals and achievements rather than the long-run building of a new culture.

While this ideal paradigm is loaded with political and economic dimensions, I'm convinced that fundamentally it is about raising the level of consciousness of each of us as individuals and through this process of society generally. Consciousness means spirit, which has something to do with such values as love, compassion, empowerment, and justice. It is embodied in the perennial wisdom that is linked to all religions and paths of wisdom.

Comprehending this paradigm of the alternative community requires a process of learning that assumes both inner development, as our spiritual growth unfolds to higher levels of actualization, and the development of a knowledge base that provides essential technical skills and institutional structures. Thus, in essence, the alternative community is a learning operation that can take an infinite variety of forms and methods.

For obvious reasons, living in an alternative community is very hard because it involves commitment to a vision, a paradigm that challenges most of the values and models of our dominant culture. It is a huge step when a person commits him/herself in this direction. The idealism that brings us into community, which means leaving behind much of the culture we're used to, is easily shattered when we quickly find that while the vision itself is extra-ordinary, the people in the community are themselves ordinary. Thus there is the gap of expectations not realized—and the challenge of how to create and implement an environment with ordinary people for this extra-ordinary goal. It's easy to get frustrated and angry, especially if and when we feel what we found in this experiment is not always working out as we had hoped. Then it's easy to assign responsibility for this seeming failure, but preferably not to ourselves.

My sense is that the alternative community at the times when it seems to be working—and those times do exist—offers a "high" because it does represent a vision being realized. But when the challenges become acute as the gap between vision and reality appears insurmountable, it's easy to wonder: Why am I doing this, what am I here for? Given the human condition, this vision is pure rhetoric and unworkable. . . .

My personal feeling, after reflecting on our High Wind experience, is that the first step is to *redefine alternative community*. The "community" does not necessarily have to be a residential enclave. My perception of High Wind is that it has always been two communities: the small nucleus of people who lived on the property near Plymouth, *and* the larger orbit of people associated with High Wind over the years who share or shared the vision to various degrees. The High Wind survey demonstrates that there is a sizable cluster of people who in many ways share the values discussed here and who benefited from the experience. I believe they represent only a fraction of others who took the vision seriously who may not have been included in the survey.

I would like to envisage a primary High Wind goal for us today: to expand the circle of people who share the vision. The beginning nucleus is the High Wind board itself. Its mission is to enlarge the concept of community, which, for our purposes, is to contribute to building a sustainable world.

So, in response to the question of whether I would want to live again in a community, my emphatic answer is *YES*, but as part of a community as here defined—not a tiny residential enclave but an association of those who commit to the shared vision.

Reflections ON THE APPEAL OF HIGH WIND
AND THE CHALLENGES OF LIVING IN COMMUNITY FROM LISA PAULSON

The reason for High Wind, its gift to participants, was not that it offered a Utopia, a more perfect society where everyone was supported and became happier, more fulfilled. Instead, its value was that people came more quickly to personal insights; their growth was speeded up because their lessons were thrown at them squarely, and they were forced to look at and deal with them.

— *2005 High Wind Survey of High Wind residents*

There's always a gap between vision and reality. Those who come with particular expectations may become frustrated; if they expect complete freedom, they'll experience restriction; if seeking structure and direction, they may find themselves uncomfortably left to their own initiatives. . . .
It goes without saying that societal transformation starts with individual well-being. People may come fired up about one and then will realize they need to embrace the other, too. Both are valued equally at High Wind, both are necessary. "Sustainable Development" gets back to discovering through the small-scale trial and error experiments of micro-societies what really can work— human to human, human to environment.

— *In an editorial "Why Does High Wind Exist?" Windwatch, Fall/Winter 1988*

Often it wasn't so much the perfection of our experiments that moved and drew people (because we and our experiments were far from perfect) but just the fact we were here and we believed in possibilities. We had seen that there was something beyond clawing our way up the job ladder for an entire lifetime, or running simply to stay in place.

— *At a High Wind board retreat, "The High Wind Myth," 1996*

It's vitally important to many of us to feel we're creating our own "thing," that we're in charge of our lives, that we're truly independent. Communities, which tend to draw people who already are stepping out from the crowd, are predicated, however, on cooperation and consensus decision-making, a sense of groupness. Very soon this mode or process starts to conflict with the personal need for individuation. As time goes by, these community members will move from a stage of throwing themselves heart and soul into the purposes and work of the group to pulling back and seeking more privacy and autonomy. They may also become tired out from giving constantly to the whole or being available to an insatiably curious public they see encroaching too much on their time. So they leave.

— *Windwatch, Spring/Summer 1989*

Bel and I were trying hard to be equals [with everyone in the community]. You say young people today are "crying for authentic adults." Perhaps our mistake was that we tried to be one of them (our young volunteers) and didn't play the part of "elders." Some said later we should have honestly acknowledged who we were, what we could give, and should have *told* the group what to do. There were no clear lines of command.

     — In response to questions from Redmoonsong, October 2002

All of us *are* deeply spiritual in sometimes unspoken ways. The sacred intent was spelled out clearly from the beginning, yet it was the physical "form-level" projects, particularly the bioshelter, that were the principle magnets that drew some of us. Our task, as the bioshelter nears completion, is to work more consciously to integrate our highest visions with the powerful energy that our physical projects evoke at the other end of the spectrum. It means strengthening our "middle" or the "glue" connecting these two, which, in turn, will define the being of High Wind as growing toward wholeness and stature.

     — Windwatch, May 1983

Milestones in the Evolution of High Wind

1976

- After spending three weeks at Findhorn, Lisa Paulson feels compelled to take back to the United States the principles guiding the Findhorn community: "restoring the balance between people and nature."

1977

- Lisa presents a workshop on Findhorn at an appropriate technology conference in Chicago and draws 400 people, which catches the attention of Belden Paulson's dean at University of Wisconsin-Extension. Bel begins to offer university courses on these concepts. (The keynote at the conference was given by *Small is Beautiful* author Fritz Schumacher.)
- Angelynn Brown arrives from Findhorn to live with Lisa and Bel and helps them promote Findhorn ideals in Wisconsin with slide shows and study groups.
- Findhorn founders Peter and Eileen Caddy arrive in Milwaukee, attracting 1,200 at a UW-Milwaukee (UWM) talk. Soon after, Lorian Association leaders (who were formerly at Findhorn) come to present a series of workshops. These events provide a critical mass that will become the constituency for ongoing, university-related courses.

- Bel organizes new courses through UWM on new paradigm, futures-oriented topics. The first major course, "Planetary Survival and the Role of Alternative Communities," attracts 125 students. These courses lay the groundwork for the creation of High Wind.
- The Paulsons dedicate the use of their rural property near Plymouth, Wisconsin, to unfolding the work of High Wind.
- The nascent group incorporates as High Wind Association, a nonprofit entity focusing on both demonstrating and educating about the themes of New Age spirituality and sustainable living.

1978

- A second major course, "New Dimensions in Governance," is sponsored by UWM, attracting 70 participants.
- Bel accompanies Lisa to Findhorn, his first exposure to that community.

- The Lorians move to Milwaukee to teach and help further conceptualize and organize High Wind.
- Lisa puts out the first issue of *Windwatch,* the High Wind newsletter, for a growing constituency.

1979

- Lisa takes a group of 23 to Findhorn for a two-month, in-depth study program sponsored by High Wind and UWM.

1980

- A second High Wind/University study group travels to Findhorn.
- High Wind applies to the U.S. Department of Energy for a grant to construct an innovative, passive solar bioshelter, modeled on the work of the Massachusetts-based New Alchemy Institute.

1981

- High Wind receives the government grant and calls a meeting to recruit volunteers to build the bioshelter on its land in Plymouth.
- A work crew coalesces; some members decide to move to the farm in Plymouth— the "intentional community" is born. By the end of the year, there are a dozen residents.
- Many educational programs begin at the High Wind site, including what is to become an annual summer seminar with members of the Lorian Association.
- Ground is broken at High Wind for construction of the bioshelter.

1982

- The Paulsons return to Findhorn to participate in the conference "Building a Planetary Village" and present a workshop about High Wind.

1984

- High Wind and UWM cosponsor the first Living/Learning Seminar in Three Communities, which consists of a small group spending a month each at High Wind, at Sirius (in Massachusetts), and at Findhorn.
- High Wind Books & Records opens in Milwaukee to bring alternative thought and materials to the city and to interface with the High Wind activity in Plymouth.
- High Wind Associates (supporters) form the High Wind Land Company to buy 20 acres west of the farmhouse, saving the land from outside development.
- The construction of the first private solar house on the High Wind ridge begins; two other homes go up over the next two years.

1986

- The second Three-Community Seminar is held at High Wind, at Eourres (in France), and at Findhorn.
- High Wind buys 62 acres east of the current property, bringing key people into its orbit who buy parcels; the entire valley is thus preserved.
- Delegates from High Wind, Sirius, the International Center for Integrative Studies

(ICIS), and Findhorn gather at UWM over a two-week period to brainstorm the question: "What implications could alternative projects have for public policy?"

1987

- A national gathering, "New Synthesis Think Tank: Laying the Groundwork—An Invitational Dialogue," convenes at the U.N. Plaza in New York. It is sponsored by High Wind, Sirius, ICIS, and Findhorn for the purpose of bringing together the best thinking of the mainstream contemporary paradigm with the best of the alternative paradigm.

1988

- Lisa and Bel attend the Findhorn conference "The Individual and the Collective"; Bel heads a panel on the alternative think tank concept.
- The first Midwest Summer Institute, comprised of diverse Wisconsin groups giving a variety of workshops, is held at High Wind.

1989-1990

- A second Midwest Summer Institute is held, again based at High Wind.

1991

- High Wind decides to let go of its "intentional community" identity to allow more independence and privacy for the residents; it continues as the High Wind Learning Center.

1992

- Some High Wind members, along with others who are not directly involved in High Wind, buy the Silver Springs property adjacent to High Wind to use for conferences and education.
- Two new corporations are created: the non-profit Plymouth Institute and the for-profit Silver Springs of Plymouth.
- High Wind receives a contract to offer programs for Milwaukee Public School students. Seven hundred inner city middle school kids come to High Wind and the Plymouth Institute for educational programs over the next few years.

1996

- A model ecovillage, SpringLedge, is designed at Silver Springs. It is nationally recognized as a sustainability pilot. The local township shoots it down and it never materializes.

1998

- Bel and Lisa return to Scotland to speak at Findhorn's annual fall conference "Ecovillages and Sustainable Communities" describing their thwarted ecovillage experiment.

1999

- The Silver Springs property is sold, to be stewarded by the Department of Natural Resources.
- High Wind sells its remaining property to residents and friends, including Peter and

Bernadette Seely, who have already established (in 1988) one of the first Community Supported Agriculture (CSA) projects in the Midwest.

2000

- The High Wind Board of Directors decides to sell its public buildings along with some of the land that surrounds them.

2001

- Richard Brandon, a Japanese Zen Buddhist leader from Chicago, buys the farmhouse/barn/coop complex. The meditation center Bright Dawn is created.

2002

- Alan Anderson and Sue Firer, Tibetan Shambhala Buddhists from Milwaukee, buy the bioshelter. They establish Windhorse, a center for retreats and classes.

2005

- The High Wind Board of Directors sends a questionaire to 180 people, nationwide, who had either lived in the community or had been involved in related activities over the 25-year span of High Wind's ongoing work.

After the sale of its property to the Zen Buddhists and the Shambhala Buddhists, the High Wind Board of Directors continues to function and creates the High Wind Foundation. This new foundation actively supports sustainability efforts in the region by awarding small grants using funds that had been derived from selling its buildings. In 2010, Bob Pavlik, longtime High Wind board member, is named executive director of the High Wind Board of Directors. The board continues to explore future directions for the High Wind Foundation while also supporting sustainability initiatives throughout Southeastern Wisconsin.

Those who had built or bought homes at High Wind continue into the present as closely connected friends in their "eco-neighborhood."

A new logo was created when Plymouth Institute began in 1992. The logo symbolizes the many interconnected initiatives of Plymouth Institute and High Wind that promote sustainable living, spiritual awareness, and alternative education. It continues to serve as the official logo of High Wind.

The Perennial Quest for "The Good Life"

An Overview of the Early History of Intentional Communities

THE VISIONARY FEW

For centuries, perhaps from the beginning of time, there have always been a few who saw inconsistencies in society, things that didn't work well. They thought if they went apart, separated out, they could create manageable, micro-examples of what an ideal society could be.

One of the earliest known actual communities was created by the Greek philosopher/scientist Pythagoras who brought his religious brotherhood to southern Italy for "moral reformation" in 529 B.C.E.

It was some four hundred years before Christ that Plato described in his *Republic* an ideal or "good" city, one with very high ethical standards, where justice was key. He advocated a communal structure within an elite ruling class—with property held in common by its citizens, including by women and children.

Then in the second century B.C.E., an ascetic Jewish sect in Palestine called the Essenes moved to the desert to form a "conscious community" that would be centered around loving and healing. They were searching for moral certainty when the old values in the cities were falling to looser standards. The Essenes were passionate about learning, had a

rigorous work ethic, prayed a lot, and were mostly celibate and deliberately money-less. Their goal was to live without greed, anger, jealousy, and lust. They were the ones who wrote the Dead Sea Scrolls and provided the basis for many of the Christian ideas that were to come later.

It is this search for a purer way to live that has inspired "intentional communities" (as distinct from random neighborhoods) throughout history—although contemporary groups might say, rather, that they are focusing on values not widely emphasized in the broader society. Here are some examples:

We note the early proliferation of Christian monasteries in remote areas to avoid persecution by the Romans. Then in the Dark Ages, various religious enclaves sprang up in response to general societal ills; these became the model for heretical communal groups to realize the teachings of Jesus on Earth. In the sixth century, St. Benedict established his rule for all the Christian monasteries that followed. Their focus was hospitality and service to the surrounding community and to the world. They reestablished schools and agricultural practices that had collapsed.

When the Seljuk empire broke down around the eighth and ninth centuries, Sufi orders of Islamic mysticism removed themselves for self-perfection and created ashrams for education and service. They espoused the Oneness of Being, believing there is no reality but God.

In the eleventh century, the Cathars, a heretical Christian sect, emerged in France, preaching a dualism where Good and Evil had separate creators for the spiritual and material worlds—similar to the Gnostic groups of the earliest Christians. Espousing equality of the sexes, they focused on charity work and were rumored to hold a secret spiritual treasure that was never discovered. Opposing almost every dictate of the Catholic Church, they were condemned in the thirteenth century by Pope Innocent III, whose army, by the end of the following century, had eradicated them as heretics.

The Waldensians were believed to be founded in twelfth-century France by a man named Valdes. While beginning as a Christian spiritual movement, they subsequently opposed the institutions of the Church of Rome, following a simple apostolic faith and promoting poverty and social justice. In the fifteenth century, they moved to the mountains of northern Italy; then, discriminated against, they were nearly wiped out in the seventeenth century. Eventually the Waldensians became some of the first Protestants.

In the mid-fifteenth century, the Unity of Brethren (Moravians) were forming in central Europe—strongly anti-Catholic and following what they felt were practices of early Christianity. Later they came to North America to found enclaves in Pennsylvania and North Carolina. There they created planned communal groupings that specialized in skilled craftsmanship. Bible study, mission work, and ideas of equality and love toward all were central.

Sir (Saint) Thomas More was certainly influenced by Plato's thinking when he wrote *Utopia* in 1516 and thus coined the term that has come down through the centuries. He described an imaginary island nation with a perfected, if unachievable, society. Order and discipline provided the basis for a culture where there was no private property and where a clear hierarchy held Christian groups together in harmony. He opposed the fragmentation of the Reformation movement, and atheists were not to be tolerated. Unlike Plato, More's family unit was central, but both of them condoned slavery.

The Anabaptist movement began in 1525 in Zurich and later became prominent in England. The Anabaptists represented the extreme element of the Reformation, questioning the long-accepted idea of masters and servants. They felt that all goods must be held in common. They also believed that moral perfection of man on earth was possible and that sin would then be no more. The Hutterites, Baptists, Quakers, and Mennonites grew out of the Anabaptists, none of which were involved with politics. They believed in complete separation between church and state, and that individuals were accountable only to God. Many were burned at the stake as heretics.

In North America, the roots of community were already established centuries before the first groups of settlers arrived from Europe to seek a more amenable way of life. For example, by the 1500s, the five major tribes in the Northeast had joined to form the Iroquois Confederacy. They created a constitution decreeing religious freedom and instituted a system of checks and balances later adopted by the founding fathers of the United States when they wrote our own Constitution.

We can say that when the Pilgrims came to America to avoid persecution during the Protestant Reformation of seventeenth century Europe, they were further examples of select groups opting to step out of the mainstream to find freedom to ground their own beliefs and values in the New World. Their settlements were intentional communities.

The Shakers—English Pietists—were one of these groups, arriving in New York State in 1774 and reaching a peak around 1826 with eighteen villages. With an absolute dedication to celibacy, the sect declined fairly rapidly—though, at this writing, I understand there may be four followers still alive in Maine. We associate the Shakers with the simple, pure lines of their furniture, and also for their practice of speaking in tongues and rhythmic dance or ecstatic trance, which they felt induced the gift of prophesy.

> The job of leaders is to illuminate and motivate.
> — *Richard Thieme, author/ philosopher, during a visit to High Wind, 1994*

The nineteenth century in the United States saw a flurry of experiments that, later, Karl Marx called "Utopian Socialism."

Father George Rapp, another Pietist, believing in devotion and repentance, rather than doctrine or works, came with a group from Germany to Pennsylvania in 1803, then moved to western Indiana on the Wabash River in 1814, where he created a prosperous (and celibate) town. Later he sold it to the Scotsman Robert Owen, who called it New Harmony. (Although the community, with examples of

peaceful cooperation, Christian morality, and love, lasted only eighteen months, its influence was felt long afterwards.)

The Owenites, fearing industrialism, created a basically socialist community, emphasizing science, education, and equality. However, they failed because they were so restricted; members revolted against the enforcement of celibacy and having to pool goods. They were also so isolated that it was hard for them to make a dent in the mainstream. The village of New Harmony exists today as a museum, with some of the original buildings preserved. I visited there in the 1990s and was invited to tea with Robert Owen's granddaughter, Jane (she wanted to know about Findhorn), an older lady who rode around town in her horse and buggy and financed good Christian works.

Charles Fourier was a Frenchman, whose theory of "passional attraction" was defined as a natural drive, stronger than reason or duty. He thought that if the drive were satisfied, harmony would result. He designed "phalanxes" of 1,620 people divided into tribes—large enough to provide a variety of passions and to express what Fourier thought was a natural order of society and human nature. His ideas migrated to the United States in the mid-nineteenth century, where several groups were started: one in Red Bank, New Jersey, that lasted twelve years, and several others in Wisconsin that lasted for five years. One of the Wisconsin sites was at Silver Springs, which was part of the Plymouth Institute property for a while.

Brook Farm, near Boston, began in 1841 with a group of noted Transcendentalists, headed by

151

Ralph Waldo Emerson and George Ripley, but they had questions about Unitarianism and the prevailing social order. Fourier had died in 1837, but the remaining Transcendentalists were intrigued by his ideas and turned Brook Farm into a phalanx, stressing communal living, education, nature, and beauty. Although the group fell on hard times and shut down after only six years, it is remembered as the most famous of the Fourier settlements. Fourier's ideas—rejection of the traditional family and religion in favor of collective enclaves where work could be pleasurable rather than demeaning; embracing of sexual freedom and equality of women; as well as recognition of the soul behind the mind—all found resonance in the radical societal changes that commenced in the 1960s in the U.S.

A number of other experiments sprang up in New England. One of the better known was the Oneida community founded by John Noyes in Putney, Vermont, in 1841. When the group was persecuted for its strangeness (including nudity), members fled to upstate New York. On joining, members had to give up all their assets. They lived a simple, vegetarian life, making decisions by consensus. They called themselves "Perfectionists" for a perfect relationship with God, one another, their community, and their work. Best known for their practice of "complex marriage," all members shared themselves sexually. For twenty years, they avoided having children (the men were in charge of birth control by abstaining from ejaculation); then they began eugenic breeding. Fifty-two children were born to selected parents and

raised communally. But then, as was/is often the case when a group is subject to rigid rules or an authoritarian leader, the community became corrupted; Noyes was accused of dictatorship and the rape of virgins. However, although the community has long since dissolved, its business of Oneida silverplate still thrives.

In 1842, Amana was started near Buffalo and then moved to Iowa. Originating in Germany, members called themselves a "community of inspiration" and became one of the longest-lived of the American experiments. It remained communal until 1932, when a decision was made to become capitalist; they divided the property and each member had his own livelihood. Today tourists may visit the Amana Heritage Society, now a historic landmark with seven villages and shops and reenactments. The group has always been noted for its fine craftsmanship and the "home-made" quality of its products. The early crafts included tinsmithing, blacksmithing, woodworking, carpet weaving, bookbinding, and printing. Businesses that thrive today sell quality appliances such as refrigerators, freezers, and air conditioners.

The oldest, largest, and most thriving of the communal societies in North America was the Hutterites. Rejecting child baptism, they formed "communities of love" in sixteenth century Austria and Moravia, then fled to Ukraine, then Switzerland to escape persecution. In 1874, four hundred of them came to South Dakota and Canada, and now they have over two hundred agricultural "colonies," with a population of some 22,000. They stress self-sufficiency and pacifism. The Bruderhof, founded in 1920, are affiliated with the Hutterites but remain a separate group.

The utopian movement, however, generally waned after the Civil War, and there was a lull in such experiments for a while.

Coming into the twentieth century, prime examples of intentional communities were the kibbutzim in what is now Israel. These started with groups from Russia after the failure of the Russian Revolution in 1905. They espoused theories of abolishing money and hired labor, with everyone living in mutual cooperation.

SOME THOUGHTS ON THE CONTEMPORARY COMMUNITY MOVEMENT

The community movement in the early part of the twentieth century—if the movement did indeed exist—remained below the radar, at least in the U.S. It wasn't until the unrest in the 1960s that young people started forming identifiable residential groups that separated out from the mainstream—to protest what they perceived to be stultified or wrong-headed societal values, or to flaunt collectively a freedom to do anything they wanted, or to live together more simply and self-reliantly. A number followed the example of Scott and Helen Nearing who moved "back to the land" in New England in the 1930s to pursue the title of one of their many books, *Living the Good Life*.

These recent decades—the '60s, '70s, and '80s—were probably the most relevant for High Wind, providing many of our root ideas that are characterized in Chapter Three, "The Contemporary Community Movement."

Appendix Three

Respondents to the 2005 High Wind Survey

HIGH WIND RESIDENTS

Joy Decker, former resident at High Wind, was responsible for the exacting job of guest program logistics; welcoming the public with warmth and enthusiasm was her trademark.

Jim Kennard, inventor extraordinaire, came from Michigan to live and work with us as High Wind morphed into Plymouth Institute, with its multiple dreams of new technological models.

David Lagerman, as a cofounder, was committed to moving to the country to anchor High Wind's mission even before the grant came through to build the bioshelter. His curiosity about higher consciousness and dedication to sharing knowledge about sustainability is legendary, and he continues to be an exemplary good neighbor in our eco-neighborhood and beyond.

Louise Mann came to live at High Wind in 1989 and married co-founder/resident David Lagerman. A compassionate "people person," she now teaches piano in her studio at High Wind and troubleshoots computer problems for all of us in the community.

Karina Martens came to live with her mother, Joann Martens, at High Wind, where everyone savored her qualities as a delightful free spirit and quick learner. She now lives with her professor husband and daughter in Texas, and works as an artist, Webmaster, and nanny.

Joann Martens was a community member and leader for several years. Joann was pivotal in organizing the community and coalescing its spiritual energy as well as shepherding the Three-Community Seminar abroad. She later married High Wind resident John Reeves, moving to Colorado where they built their own ecologically-inspired home.

HIGH WIND PROGRAM LEADERS

Bethe Hagens, anthropology researcher/professor, exuberant violinist, and free spirit, played a major role in the early period of Plymouth Institute/Silver Springs. She now lives near the ocean in Maine and mentors at Goddard College in Vermont.

Wil Kraegel, futurist professor at UW-Milwaukee, was active with Bel Paulson in the World Future Society chapter of Milwaukee and has

155

been a longtime supporter of High Wind and its goals.

Milenko Matanovic, Lorian leader, came to teach with us for six years in Wisconsin. As we began to formulate High Wind, he held our hands and gave constant, wisely critical advice. Currently his mission is coalescing urban groups to create projects that foster beauty, utility, and community through Pomegranate Center that he founded and directs.

Tom McGinnity, High Wind board member and indefatigable educator in the Milwaukee Public Schools, was instrumental in facilitating the program bringing seven hundred inner city kids to High Wind from Grand Avenue Middle School, where he was principal.

Bob Pavlik is a creative professor of education at Marquette University, a High Wind board member, and one of our strongest and most sensitive supporters. He has been an important spiritual touchstone for all of us working with High Wind projects. His influence has also been felt throughout the greater Milwaukee area and beyond.

Barbara Prendergast (senior) is a board member and was a frequent coordinator or leader of programs at High Wind as well as the trips abroad. A regional leader of the Centering Prayer initiative, she always provides perceptive spiritual ballast for us.

Freya Secrest has been a strong member of the Lorian Association from its start in the early 1970s. For several years, she lived in our area, and, bringing her experience and wisdom to

bear, assumed the presidency of High Wind to steer us through some major, tricky organizational changes. She now lives in Seattle, where she is active in creating learning programs with the Lorian group based there.

PARTICIPANTS IN HIGH WIND PROGRAMS

Kesha Engel was an ebullient seventeen-year-old when she came to our earliest classes; she continued to participate in High Wind programs over the years, and is currently active in healing and spiritual work.

Beth Herbert was an early cheerleader for High Wind. After going on the 1979 trip to Findhorn, she visited the community frequently, bringing her unique brand of raucous enthusiasm and fabulous cooking skills, which greatly buoyed everybody's spirits.

Elizabeth Matson participated in the 1984 Living/Learning Seminar in Three Communities and, as a writer and storyteller, she chronicled the trip for her group. She came for subsequent events at High Wind and had hoped to join the Thistledown ecovillage, which didn't materialize. She now lives, studies, and works in Arizona.

Susan Newstead first met us at the Chicago Schumacher environmental conference in 1977, went on to join our trip to Findhorn in 1979, and then became a regular at the summer Lorian-High Wind seminars into the 1980s. She lives in California and produces public radio programs.

Judith Pintar was an insightful, energetic, creative teenage participant in our early classes who signed up for our first group trip to Findhorn in 1979. Now, with a family and several books under her belt, she's a sociology professor in Illinois. In retrospect, partly as a result of her own searing research experiences in Bosnia, her conclusion is that our visions in the 1970s didn't go far enough.

Barbara Prendergast (junior), a teacher at the Urban Waldorf School in Milwaukee, was a long-time participant in many High Wind programs, including the Three-Community Seminar.

Susan Safran, a teacher who came up regularly from Chicago to our Lorian-High Wind summer seminars in the early years, has been an enthusiastic supporter.

Pamm Steffen came into High Wind's orbit in the early 1990s and found ways to mesh what she found there with her teaching at Mt. Mary College in Milwaukee and her involvement with local architects and with the Midwest Renewable Energy Association.

Robert Thompson participated in most of the early activities at High Wind, including the 1979 trip to Findhorn. He lives in New York with his wife and son, writes poetry, and commutes by bike to teach college English.

John Weaver came from Michigan to attend many of our summer Lorian-High Wind seminars and, over the years, has entertained us with his incisive, humorous monologues and tracts.

Alan Zuberbuehler participated in various High Wind activities and served on the board of High Wind Books. He paints houses, writes plays, and does impersonations.

Metka Zupancic, since moving to the U.S. from her native Slovenia, has sought a spiritual home and confreres. She found her way to our summer Lorian-High Wind seminars and teaches yoga, philosophy, literature, and myth at the University of Alabama. Recently she was knighted in France for her contributions and scholarship.

About the Author

Writer Lisa Paulson grew up along the East Coast of the United States. From early on, she had looked beyond the mainstream and felt compelled to challenge status quo trends and values. She saw the imperative for different cultures to stand in each others' shoes, and then to bring such exercises down to the micro level. She recognized that a truly sustainable way of life is best realized in the cooperation of groups such as "intentional communities"—relatively manageable entities whose members try to live out a particular vision.

In 1952, with backpack and idealism, Lisa landed in southern Italy, where she was to live off and on for the next nine years. In Naples, she met and worked with Belden Paulson, who had created Casa Mia, a settlement center for homeless Neapolitans displaced by World War II. The couple married in 1954. In the fall of 1957, Lisa, Bel, and their eleven-month-old son Eric returned to Italy to spearhead a project to resettle Iron Curtain refugees on the island of Sardinia. They remained in Sardinia for two years and then moved to Rome, where Bel worked with the United Nations to implement a plan to resettle the remaining refugees in Italian camps. While in Rome, their son Steve was born. The family moved to Wisconsin in the fall of 1962.

Between 1976 and 1998, Lisa made a number of extended visits to the Findhorn Foundation near Inverness in northeast Scotland—the renowned community modeling new ways of living and thinking and being. These trips, along with her travels to learn from the technological pioneers at the New Alchemy Institute in Massachusetts, had a profound impact on her. She felt compelled to bring these ideas back to the Midwestern United

States. The result was the creation of High Wind, the intentional community she and Bel, with a group of dedicated volunteers, founded in the early 1980s—a small, rural enclave abutting the Northern Kettle Moraine State Forest in Wisconsin.

The focus of this experiment was on matters of ecology, education, and spirit. *An Unconventional Journey* documents the birth and unfolding of High Wind—the highs and lows, the challenges and achievements—and its ultimate transition from an intentional community to an ecological neighborhood.

Currently Lisa and Bel divide their time between their solar home at High Wind in Wisconsin and the countryside of Vermont.

Other Books Published by Thistlefield Books

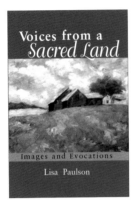

Voices from a Sacred Land
by Lisa Paulson

While chronicling the history of High Wind, an experimental ecological community developed with her husband Belden, Lisa Paulson realized that it was the powerful, enchanting, healing presence of nature itself that had deeply influenced all she felt and did. This poetic collection of her own and others' responses to the land she had grown to love and cherish is enhanced by four-color photographs and paintings. *Voices* will increase your appreciation of nature and expand your awareness of the central role of the natural world in our lives.

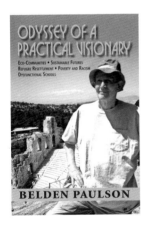

Odyssey of a Practical Visionary
by Belden Paulson

Odyssey of a Practical Visionary is the story of Belden Paulson, whose life has been dedicated to building a better world politically and economically. His many distinct careers—international, urban, futures—reflect a recurring theme: tackling problems that others often called "hopeless," sometimes with surprising results. This book is a fascinating and compelling memoir of unique experiences and brave experiments—pointing the way to a better future for the human family.

Purchase these books on the Thistlefield Books Web site: http://ThistlefieldBooks.com/
or contact Thistlefield Books at:
W7122 County Road U
Plymouth, Wisconsin 53073